# The West Coast Travel Guide

## Exploring the Islands, Towns and Byways, by Ferry, Car and Bicycle.

### David Vincent-Jones

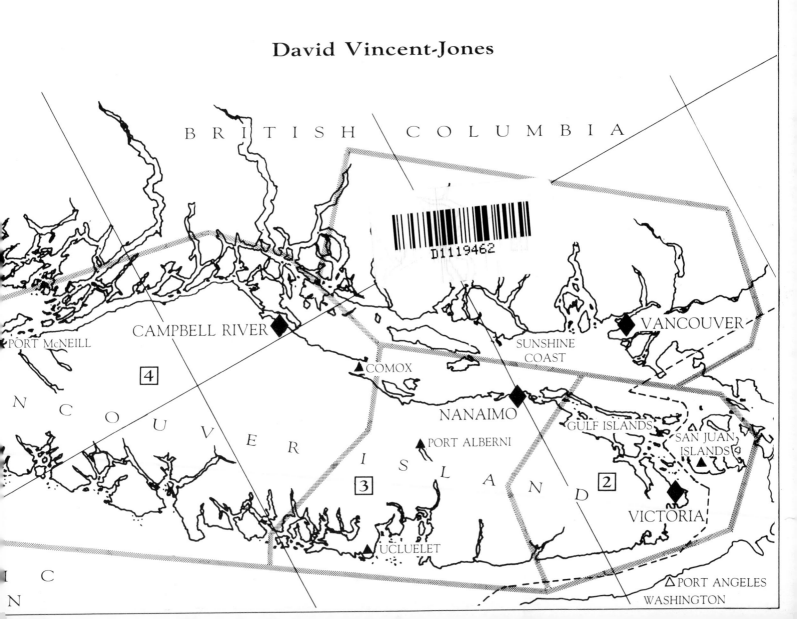

BRITISH COLUMBIA

PORT McNEILL

CAMPBELL RIVER

VANCOUVER

SUNSHINE COAST

4

COMOX

NANAIMO

V C O U V E R

GULF ISLANDS

SAN JUAN ISLANDS

PORT ALBERNI

3

I S L A N D

2

VICTORIA

UCLUELET

PORT ANGELES
WASHINGTON

Published by Coastal Publications Ltd.
Cypress House. 1904, West 16th. Avenue,
Vancouver, V6J 2M4, British Columbia.


Canadian Cataloguing in Publication Data

Vincent-Jones, David, 1934-
The West Coast Travel Guide.

ISBN 0-920551-00-9

Community and Travel Research by
Anne O'Shaughnessy
Photographs by
David Vincent-Jones, Lynn Yip and Peter Vassilopoulos
Editing by
Peter Vassilopoulos and Dianna Frid
Graphics Coordination by
Dana Cleland

Production and Design by
David Vincent-Jones


Printed in Hong Kong
by Everbest Printing Co., Ltd.

# Contents

# Vancouver and the Sunshine Coast

PERSONS USING
THESE PREMISES
DO SO AT THEIR
OWN RISK

*Expo '86, Vancouver City:*
The impetuous symmetry of this sphere forming
part of the city's Expo site captures reflections of
sun, water, and the progress of humanity.

*Savary Island: By the Landing.*
Who knows what these quiet shores have seen through the dark nights. It was towards these secluded sandy shores that the *Rumrunners* pointed their heavily laden launches during the prohibition days.

*Gibsons Landing: floating cabin*
It's hard to know just where reality ends and the film set begins in this community built by loggers and fishermen.

*One Man Band, Granville Island:*
Good humor and nostalgic tunes accompanied by
laughter are an important ingredient for the
visitors to Granville Island Public Market.

*Ruby Lake, Sechelt Peninsula.*
Sifting through the leaves, our sight reaches the
water; from its background, the mountains
emerge.

*Arbutus Tree, Sunshine Coast:*
The unusual thin skin of the Arbutus peels back
revealing its light greenish wood, almost as
smooth as it feels when touched.

*Lund Harbour.*
A sharp turn and the road ends in a quiet cove;
this is however where many exciting journeys
really start on this sun-washed shore.

*Savary Island: by the landing*
It was to be a summer retreat for the established, with grand houses, tennis courts and lots of flag poles.

*Bowen Island, Water Lilly.*
Hidden away, just a stones throw from the
roaring city's pace, an island of parks and
tranquility.

*Settlers Cabin, Powell River.*
Once an industrious dairy farm, hacked from the forest by pioneers, slowly is overtaken by modern process.

# Vancouver

Vancouver, a city to bedazzle the eyes, a city in a matchless setting, civilised but raw, at the edge of a vast untrodden mountain wilderness.

The lucky ones see Vancouver first from the water where the cityscape rises tall, floating out of the sea like a shimmering mirage and lacey Lion's Gate bridge is enveloped at it's southern end in the primeval green of Stanley Park, a largely untouched one-thousand acre coastal forest preserve right within the city's downtown core. In the foreground of English Bay, freighters and barges piled high, cautiously feel their

*The view of Vancouver as seen from the beautiful gardens at Queen Elizabeth Park while the sun begins to set.*

way, past bright clean sandy beaches and rocky coves, punctuated by a flotilla of pleasure boats of every shape and size.

This city's life, with its cosmopolitan outlook, mild climate and delights to satisfy even the most jaded traveller, has been the envy of many a visitor, regardless of where they have come from. The often-told stories of skiing in the morning and swimming or playing a few holes of golf in the afternoon are very much a reality and many of the office towers afford tantalisingly close views over both the beaches and ski slopes.

Geographically, the city is water-fragmented, with harbours, inlets, rivers and bays protruding not only into the land mass but into the very way of life of its inhabitants. The Marine Building, Vancouver's first 'skyscraper', conjures the very essence of the dynamic maritime growth through the early years and is a magnificent example of the art of the last generation of builders, as is today's Canada Place complex, decked with monumental sweeping silvery sails to welcome the arriving cruise vessels on their way to the northern waters. Downtown streets are punctuated with water views, commuters crawl to work over busy bridges or cross the harbour on the brisk bright Seabus, shoppers crowd the fresh food stands of the Granville Island Market and everyone goes to 'their own' piece of beach; the water, the beach, the open sea, it's a whole way of life. As a foil for all that water and civilization, within touching distance, the mountains start, raw, wild and empty. You could walk North for a thousand miles, or two thousand, and never see another soul.

A multicultural and seemingly nomadic population, brings to the city's daily life an extraordinary collage. It seems hard to find people born and bred locally, and the diversity of the varied cultures has hardly been softened by time. 'Chinatown', is not just a good place for tourists to eat and buy nick-nacks, it is a cohesive working commuinity in every respect in a city which has the largest percentage of Chinese per capita of any in the Western world. Similarly, Italians, Greeks, East Indians, Germans, and a wealth of other nations all bring vibrantly colourful pasts, brazenly exposed, to the expanding metropolis.

Brash, modern architecture has become the accepted norm in a young society with few ties to the past. B.C.

Place Stadium apears to lie like a great white whale, beached, and straining against its cables on the edge of False Creek, amid the glittering marinas, townhouses and the future-scape designs of the pavilions and structures of the Expo86 site. Local architect Arthur Erickson's pen has been responsible for many of today's city landmarks, transforming the turn of the century courthouse into the new Art Gallery and restructured the entire downtown core with the new Law Courts complex, a flowing glass, steel and concrete extravaganza. East of the city the Simon Fraser University sits Olympus-like high above the residences and commerce of suburban Burnaby affording students and visitors sweeping mountain and city panoramas, while on a high bluff at the western extreme the older and more traditional University of British Columbia combines the conventional ivy-clad learning structures with the new and dramatic. Locals and visitors alike sit and watch the setting sun from the Museum of Anthropology where totem poles, "long houses" and modern construction all stand together in magical harmony.

Visitors to Vancouver will easily find well organised tourist facilities, such as the numerous bus and water tours of the city and surroundings arranged through all of the city's hotels, but for many there will be an even greater pleasure in joining with the locals as they enjoy their city, with its rich cultural life and constant closeness to the enveloping nature. Take a lazy long Sea Wall walk around Stanley Park and feel the cool lush growth right in the city's heart, cruise up the harbour one evening as the sun is setting or ride the Skyride to the top of Grouse Mountain and stand at the watershed between a dynamic population and absolute wilderness to the North. The locals, will eat out seemingly at any flimsy excuse, no doubt on account of the superb selection of varied eateries to suit every taste and pocketbook. In the parks among the trees, high in the air with views that are forever, and in every segment of town the specialty restaurants thrive with temptingly delicious foods from all over the world. In the downtown core the Pacific Centre shopping mall and the surrounding streets provide sophisticated shoppers with a carnival of fashion and temptations hard to resist.

# What To Do And See:

The wealth of places to visit and things to do in the Vancouver area makes selection difficult. We offer the following random selection: – The Arts, Sciences and Technology Centre with live shows and hands-on science exhibits; B.C. Place Stadium; Harbour Centre complex with shopping mall, observation deck and revolving restaurant; Museum of Anthropolgy on the University of B.C. campus, featuring outstanding collections of Northwest Indian artifacts, B.C. and Pacific Rim archeological exhibits, and costume and textile displays; the Old Hasting Mill Store Museum, one of Vancouver's oldest buildings housing relics of the city's early days; Queen Elizabeth Park for its grand view of the city and magnificent gardens, plus the Bloedel Conservatory of tropical plants; the Vancouver Museum/Maritime Museum/MacMillan Planetarium complex in Vanier Park on English Bay; Stanley Park with its zoo, rose gardens, open air theatre, walks, trails and cycling paths, sports facilities, Children's Zoo and miniature railway, and the wonderful Vancouver Aquarium and its whale shows. The University of B.C. Botanical Gardens, and the Van Dusen Botanical Gardens together with MacMillan Bloedel Place are well worth a visit. At Exhibition Park one may enjoy thoroughbred racing, take a tour of the B.C. Pavilion and B.C. Sports Hall of Fame, or ride the roller coaster at Playland. Interesting shopping and restaurants may be found in Chinatown, Gastown (Old Vancouver), 'Robsonstrasse', and on Granville Island where its wonderful market offers fresh fruits, vegetables, seafoods, meats, gourmet items and handicrafts. The Vancouver Art Gallery contains major works of Emily Carr as well as other noteworthy exhibits. Robson Square Media Centre has a great variety of constantly changing (and often free) attractions – seminars, lectures, exhibits and concerts. The elegant old Orpheum Theatre is home to the Vancouver Symphony Orchestra, while the Vancouver Opera Company performs at the Queen Elizabeth Theatre. Stage Productions are also held at the Arts club Theatres, The playhouse Theatre, Vancouver East Cultural Centre, City Stage, Metro Theatre, and others. Out of doors theatrical and musical productions are held during the summer at both Malkin Bowl in Stanley Park, and

*above:*
*A visit to Chinatown is a visit to another cultural environment.*

*right:*
*Sidewalk cafes under the trees in Gastown.*

at Kitsilano Showboat. Vancouver is noted for its city beaches which extend from Stanley Park around English Bay and out to the University of B.C.'s campus on Point Grey. The Vancouver Parks Board provides swimming pools, tennis courts, golf and mini-golf courses, lawn bowling, archery and horseshoe pitching facilities, and cycling routes ☎ 681-1141.

Sports fans can see the B.C. Lions football team play at B.C. Place Stadium, or the Vancouver Canucks hockey team at the Pacific Coliseum. Not too far out of town attractions include the Grouse Mountain Skyride for a breathtaking view of the city, harbour and Georgia Strait; The George Reifel Bird Sanctuary in Ladner; Deer Lake Park in Burnaby featuring operating displays in the turn of the century Heritage Village Museum, craft markets and art gallery; Lynn Canyon Park for nature paths, fishing and swimming pools; and Capilano Canyon and Suspension Bridge. Local celebrations include the Children's Festival – May; Music Festival, Shakespeare Festival, Sea Festival, Folk Festival – July; B.C. Salmon Derby, Pacific National Exhibition – August: Christmas Carol Flotilla – December.

## How To Get There:

**By Car:** Trans-Canada Highway 1 from the East (Also Highways 7 and 1A); Highway 99 (U.S. I-5) from the South. **By Bus:** The Vancouver Bus Terminal is located at 150 Dunsmuir St. Grayhound Lines from the B.C. Interior and points east ☎ (Vancouver) 683-9277. Pacific Coach Lines from Vancouver Island ☎ (Vancouver) 683-9277. Trailways from Seattle ☎ (Vancouver) 872-8311. Maverick Coach Lines from Sechelt Peninsula and Squamish/Whistler ☎ (Vancouver) 255-1171. **By Train:** VIA Rail Canada, Vancouver to eastern Canada and waypoints ☎ 1-800-665-8630 toll free. British Columbia Railway,

North Vancouver to Prince George and waypoints ☎ (Vancouver) 987-6216.

**By Boat:** B.C. Ferries, Vancouver to Nanaimo (Vancouver Island) and Sechelt Peninsula depart terminal at Horseshoe Bay (21 km northwest of Vancouver). B.C. Ferries Vancouver to Victoria and the Gulf Islands depart from the terminal at Tsawwassen (35 km south of Vancouver). **By Air:** Vancouver International Airport is located on Sea Island approximately 15 km south of Vancouver off Highway 99. Airporter buses operate to and from major downtown hotels from 6 a.m. to midnight.

## How To Get Around:

**Metro Transit:** bus service within the city and to suburban areas; also Seabus service between Vancouver city center and North Vancouver ☎ 324-3211. **The Visitors' Bureau** at Robson Square has detailed information sheets on how to visit many Vancouver attractions using public transportation. Bus tours of the city and surounding areas are offered by Gray Line ☎ 872-8311; British Double Decker Bus Tours ☎ 669-0110; and Scenic Line Mini-Bus Tours ☎ 980-4744. Scenic Line also offers a day trip to Victoria on Vancouver Island, and Gray Line has 1,2, and 3-day tours to Victoria. Pathfinder Walking Tours has 1½ hr. guided tours of sections of Old Vancouver and Chinatown ☎ 731-4882. Harbour activities can be viewed from vantage points at the foot of Granville St. (Granville Square), from Stanley Park, from the foot of Clark Drive (Vanterm), or from the Seabus which departs Granville Square at regular intervals throughout the day. A 1hr. guided tour of the port is available at Vanterm (reservations) ☎ 666-6129. A little further afield, Circle Nature Adventures offers guided walking tours (with gourmet lunches) of a variety scenic areas around Vancouver ☎ 254-5015. **Taxis:** Advance Cabs ☎ 876-5555; Black Top Cabs ☎ 681-2181; Vancouver Taxi, with preference given to wheelchair passengers ☎ 255-7322; and others. **Car Rentals:** Avis ☎ 682-1621: Budget ☎ 685-0536; Hertz ☎ 688- 2411; Rent-A-Wreck ☎ 688-0001; and more. **Boat Charters/Rentals:** Too numerous to list. Pick up a free copy of 'Boat Charters and Rentals' and/or 'Canoeing' from the Visitors' Bureau.

**Boat tours** of Vancouver Harbour (1¼ hrs.) or to Ganville Island (4hrs) are offered by Harbour Ferries Ltd. ☎ 687-9558. A 15 min. ferry ride may be taken from Granville Island to the Planetarium/Museums complex ☎ 681-8621, or a short trip may be made from Vancouver's West End (behind the Aquatic Centre at 1050 Beach) to Granville Island ☎ 734-2082. The MV Britannia departs downtown Vancouver for a day-cruise up Howe Sound to Squamish; and the *Royal Hudson* steam engine travels the same route along the scenic coast. The two tours can be combined for a delightful boat and rail round trip. For information

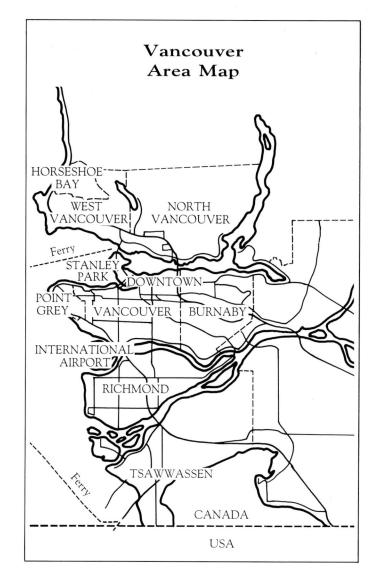

**Vancouver Area Map**

HORSESHOE BAY
WEST VANCOUVER
NORTH VANCOUVER
Ferry
STANLEY PARK
DOWNTOWN
POINT GREY
VANCOUVER
BURNABY
INTERNATIONAL AIRPORT
RICHMOND
Ferry
TSAWWASSEN
CANADA
USA

and reservations ☎ 687-9558. **Bicycle Rentals:** Bayshore Bicycles ☎ 689-5071, and Stanley Park Rentals ☎ 681-5581 are both located on West Georgia Street close to Stanley Park. Also Bikes on Broadway ☎ 874-8611; or Dunbar Cycles ☎ 783-7022, and others. **Diving Rentals:** Adrenilin Sports, Granville Island ☎ 682-2881; Capilano Divers Supply, North Vancouver ☎ 986-4646; Odyssey Diving Centre ☎ 430-1451; and others. **Windsurfer Rentals:** Wind Tech ☎ 681-8324; Sportif ☎ 736-6411. **White water rafting** trips are available on the Chilliwack, Fraser and Thompson Rivers by Whitewater Adventures ☎ 669-1100; Hyak River Expeditions ☎ 734-8622, and others.

*Frothy fountains and the New Art Gallery at the City Centre.*

## Where To Stay And Eat:

**Hotels and motels** are available in a seemingly endless list, through every standard and price range. The oldest of the downtown established hotels, modernised but still with much grace and character is the centrally located Vancouver Hotel ☎ 684-3131. On the edge of False Creek, by Stanley Park, with fine water-front vistas is the Bayshore Inn ☎ 682-3377. For those wishing to stay on the north side of the harbour the Park Royal Hotel ☎ 926-5511 in West Vancouver is intimate and secluded while being close to the action of downtown. The alternatives boggle the mind and visitors would be well advised to call Res-West ☎ 688-0044 for a free computerised hotel reservation system to ease the dificulty.

**Eating out** in Vancouver is a true treat for visitors with a depth and range of food types rarely found elsewhere. Here, with literally thousands to choose from, we can only single out a very few; not, by the way, in any special order, to wet your appetite. Northern Italian in an enchanting garden ☎ 669-2422 Il Giardino; a Japanese Sushi bar ☎ 689-7351 Koji's; light modern cuisine with flair ☎ 734-1325 Mark James; char-grilled salmon, with a great view ☎ 926-3212 The Salmon House; sea food, pasta and entertainment while you eat ☎ 736-8828 Mama Golds; an old established steak house ☎ 683-7671 Hy's Encore; dim sum for lunch ☎ 872-2644 Fairyland Chinese Seafood Resturant. Reservations are recomended for all of these resturants. For those wanderers in search of food, try the length of Robson street, Pender street in the Chinatown district, or three blocks north in Gastown, there are many many superb and inexpensive eateries and poking around to find one that suits your taste on any one particular night can be half the fun of these areas.

**The Visitors' Bureau** offers the free booklet *Attractions on the Lower Mainland* with descriptions and pertinent information on attractions in and about Vancouver.

**Visitors' Information:** Royal Centre, 1625-1055 West Georgia St, Vancouver ☎ 682-2222.

**Air charters:** Too numerous to list. The Vancouver Visitors' Bureau has a free booklet available on Aircraft Charters and Rentals, or consult the yellow pages of the Vancouver telephone directory. Two companies offering helicopter tours in the area are Wright Brothers Aviation Ltd. ☎ 525-1484, and Nova Helicopters ☎ 273-9732.

# Howe Sound to Sechelt

Howe Sound, the change takes your breath away. So close to the city lights and city life, a deep blue slash of water framed with snow capped mountains and studded with islands of every shape and size.

Tiny protected Horseshoe Bay, packed with converging ferries, cars, bicycles and above all people on the move; cockle shell fishing dinghys and scudding power boats hurrying off to some quiet cove. Horseshoe Bay is a divide between the busy city life and tranquillity, where travellers get the first clear views of the wilderness of the Coast Range mountains with almost shear slopes that rise straight from the water to snow-capped peaks from here to the Artic Circle.

A small ferry thuds its way with day trippers and regulars over to Snug Cove on Bowen Island, a long established weekend cottage retreat that fortunately has never been greatly developed or exploited, where beautiful foreshore parks, woods and lakes are just a few minutes walk from the island ferry terminal and the few small clap-boarded stores, show signs of a community pride while still looking as they would have looked fifty years ago.

On the west side of the sound, after twisting among the islands, a second ferry lands at Langdale; close by, Gibsons Landing, a fishing and logging village lies tucked into a small rocky cove close to the southern entrance to the Sunshine Coast. Here everyday life mingles with the on-going filming activities of a television series in the downtown streets and along the colourful harbour floats. Its hard to tell in this town, where the actors are often the locals, just where reality ends and the fantasy of the set begins.

A tortuous highway, providing a real treat for the eyes, winds its way over deep rushing ravines and under shear rock faces along the eastern side of the sound, past the now disused copper mines at Britannia Beach, to where the town of Squamish huddles at the base of the 'Chieftain', a 600 metre vertical wall of rock, an awe-inspiring rock climber's mecca. The copper mines now have been turned into the B.C.Mining Museum, where visitors can really taste the underground experience, get a feel for how minerals today are won from the ground and perhaps appreciate more the pioneers of yesteryear.

See the Sunshine Coast, page 24, for more information around the Sechelt Peninsula.

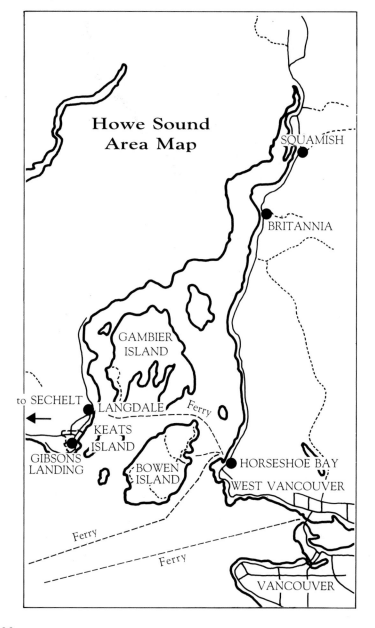

Howe Sound Area Map

*From Vancouver, Horseshoe Bay marks the entrance to beautiful Howe Sound.*

## What To See And Do

Enjoy the beaches, the excellent fishing and scuba diving. Hike the many trails — to Soames Point Lookout near Gibsons, to Skookumchuk Narrows (the Boiling Water) near Egmont, or to the waterfalls near Roberts Creek. Wilderness camping can be enjoyed by travelling the logging roads on weekends. (Check with the logging companies and information centres before using.) Visit the Limestone Caves near Halfmoon Bay. Elphinstone Pioneer Museum at Gibsons features displays of local history as well as a large shell collection. Also at Gibsons, the location for the TV series *The Beachcombers*. Take a tour of Canadian Forest Products pulp mill at Port Mellon. Golf at the Sunshine Coast Golf Course. The Hunter Gallery in Gibsons has local arts and crafts. Local celebrations include Sechelt Timber Days — May; Gibsons Sea Cavalcade — August; and the Arts and Crafts Fair at the Arts Centre in Sechelt — August. There are two weekly newspapers — The Sunshine Coast News and The Press.

## How To Get There:

**By Car or Bicycle:** B.C. Ferries Vancouver (Horseshoe Bay) to Langdale, then along Highway 101 4 km to Gibsons, a further 23 km to Sechelt and then 39 km to Pender Harbour. Or, Ministry of Highways Ferry Comox (Vancouver Island) to Powell River, then 31 km south on Highway 101 to Saltery Bay, by B.C. Ferries Saltery Bay to Earls Cove, and then 17 km south to Pender Harbour. **By Bus:** Maverick Coach Lines from Vancouver or south from Powell River: Vancouver ☎ 255-1171. **By Air:** Tyee Airways: Sechelt ☎ 885-2214.

## How To Get Around

**Taxi:** Coast Taxi (serving the Sunshine Coast): Sechelt ☎ 885-2217. **Car Rental:** Rent-A-Wreck: Gibsons ☎ 886-9717. **Water Taxi:** Call-In Water Taxi: Sechelt ☎ 885-2100; Madeira Marina: Pender Harbour ☎ 883-2266. **Boat Charter/Rental:** Wahoo Enterprises: Gibsons ☎ 836-9351; Sunshine Coast Sailboat: Gibsons ☎ 886-3717; Davis Bay Rentals: Sechelt ☎ 885-7345; Lowes Resort Motel: Pender Hbr ☎ 883-2456; and others. **Canoe Rentals:** Lowes Resort Motel. **Diving:** Skookum Scuba: Pender Hbr ☎ 883-2302. **Boat Launch:** Gibsons Village; Irvine's Landing & Madeira Park in the Pender Harbour area; and Porpoise Bay in the Sechelt area. Others. **Riding:** Sylvan Hills Stables: Gibsons ☎ 886-2001. **Air Charter:** Tyee Airways: Sechelt ☎ 8852214.

## Where To Stay And Eat

Sunshine Lodge: Gibsons ☎ 886-3321; Driftwood Inn, with The Pebbles Restaurant: Sechelt ☎ 885-5811; Jolly Roger Inn at Halfmoon Bay, licensed restaurant: ☎ 885-7184. Provincial campgrounds at Roberts Creek, 14 km west of Gibsons; and Porpoise Bay, 4 km east of Sechelt. Silver Sands Resort, campground and trailer park: Pender Hbr ☎ 883-2630. Many others. The Wharf Restaurant in Bella Beach Motel: Sechelt ☎ 885-7285; or the restaurant at Lord Jim's Lodge at Halfmoon Bay ☎ 885-2232

**Visitor Information:** Gibsons Chamber of Commerce, Box 1190, Gibsons, V0N 1V0 ( ☎ 886-2325); or Sechelt Chamber of Commerce, Box 360, Sechelt, V0N 3A0 ( ☎ 885-3100).

# The Sunshine Coast

What a place for waterside vacations; where the low rocky, boulder strewn shores are flanked by the toothy Tantalus mountains and Native Indian legend has it that the rocks on the beaches are those that were hurled down when the spirits sawed out the mountain tops. A coastline, of slender land-ribbons, of bays, beaches, islands and most of all an access to a million quiet coves.

The ruggedness around the fjords and the use of ferries for transportation to the Sunshine Coast, makes it feel more like going to an island, even though it is part of the mainland and the ease of access to serene areas of beach and protected waters makes the Sunshine Coast a popular destination particularly for those looking for the quick escape from the bustle of Vancouver.

The town of Sechelt, in the south, provides superb small boat access to hundreds of miles of protected inland coastline and secluded inlets that connect to Jervis Inlet while a little further north the tucked-away communities like Secret Cove and Pender Harbour presents a selection of long established resorts and marinas set into deep inlets that particularly attract boaters, fishermen and the lover of the local fresh oyster. At the most northerly tip of the Sechelt Peninsula the tidal rapids at Skookumchuk Narrows are a spectacular exhibit of the forces of ocean waters, where soaring alpine crags preside over the salty turbulences.

From Earl's Cove to Saltery Bay a ferry carries passengers and cars past islands and snug summer havens through the majestic and deep black waters of Jervis Inlet, extending the road system northward to its end on the narrow Malaspina Peninsula where it thrusts out into the warmth of Desolation Sound. That forlorn-sounding name, by the way, is reported to be Captain George Vancouver's reaction when he found nothing noteworthy at the site and a lack of fish and berries to provision his men, certainly he was not remarking about the view. Powell River, an old established pulp mill town, sits at a narrow neck between Georgia Strait and the 30 mile long fresh water paradise for small boats of Powell Lake while scuba-divers, windsurfers and a host of other water lovers frequent the warm ocean shores taking advantage of the crystal clear waters.

From the fishing village of Lund, north of Powell River, Savory Island can be reached by water taxi. The island, once reputed as a base for rum-runners, was for a time an exclusive and secluded retreat for industrialists; now the grand old homes and gardens with slender flag staffs that border the wide white beaches, sit tranquilly mature with natures' cover of wild flowers, mosses and giant arbutus trees to make a perfect secluded escape for a day or a week.

A short ferry ride from Powell River takes visitors over to Blubber Bay on the elongate Texada Island. At the turn of the century Vananda, the principle island town, was the scene of a massive gold strike and for a while was the largest west coast city north of Seattle. Today three terraced limestone mines, as well an iron ore mine are the economic backbone of the island and very little of those roaring days is to be seen. Smaller scale rock-hounding is now a noted attraction of Texada and a greenish porphyrite with sparkles of white designs, called the 'Texada flower rock', is a much sort after prize. The west shore of the island has numerous beaches.

## How To Get Around:

**City Bus Transit:** ☎ 485-5030; Aero Cabs: ☎ 485-2731; Lund **Water Taxi:** ☎ 483-9749; **Car Rental:** Budget/Avis Rent-A-Car: ☎ 485-6267; Tilden Rent-A-Car: ☎ 485-2731. **Boat Charter/Rental:** Jason Marine: ☎ 485-2212; Sunset Coast Marine: ☎ 485-4727; Beach Gardens Resort Hotel: ☎ 482-6267; Smith's Canoe Outfitters: ☎ 485-2651. **Boat Launch:** Saltery Bay Picnic Site, Westview Harbour, Powell Lake and Lund. Horses: Maple Springs Ranch: ☎ 485-5202. Air Charter: Powell Air: ☎ 485-4262; Tyee Air: ☎ 482-9223.

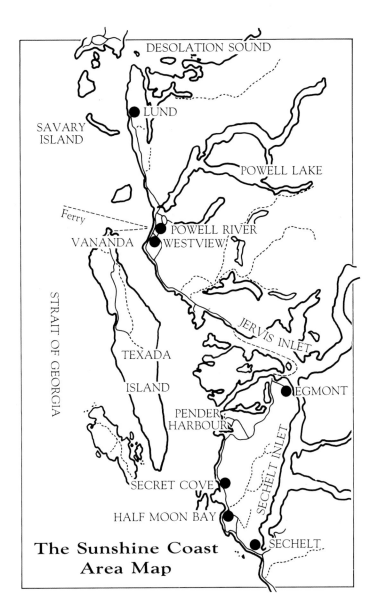

**The Sunshine Coast Area Map**

## How to Get There:

**By Car:** B.C. Ferries Vancouver (Horseshoe Bay) to Langdale (35 min), then drive 83 km along the Sechelt Peninsula to Earls Cove, then by ferry to Saltery Bay (50 min), and finally a further 31 km along to Highway 101 to Powell River. The small fishing village of Lund may be reached by travelling an additional 28 km from Powell River; or, by Ministry of Highways Ferry Comox (Vancouver Island) to Powell River (1¼ hrs). **By Bus:** Maverick Coach Lines from Vancouver via Sechelt Peninsula: Phone Vancouver ☎ 255-1171. **By Air:** Air B.C. from Vancouver or Victoria: ☎ Vancouver 685-3211; ☎ Victoria 388-5151. Tyee Airways Ltd. from Vancouver or Nanaimo: ☎ Vancouver 689-8651; Powell River 485-9223. To reach Texada Island take the Ministry of Highways Ferry from Powell River (Westview) to Blubber Bay on Texada Is. (35 min).

## What To See And Do:

The Powell River Historical Museum features local historical artifacts and displays, while the Powell River Archeological Exhibit at Willingdon Beach features the life of the Coast Salish Indians. Pulp and paper mill tours may be taken of Macmillan Bloedel Ltd. from May to September: ☎ 483-3722. The Cranberry Lake Wildlife Sanctuary is of interest as is the 1.6 km Willingdon Creek Nature Trail at Willingdon Beach. A panoramic view of Malaspina Strait may be seen by taking the hiking trail to Mt. Valentine Lookout. For the canoeist there is an 8-lake circuit with portages near Powell River. Saltery Bay Provincial Park offers fishing, swimming and excellent scuba diving as well as camping facilities. Golf at the Powell River Golf Course. Shop for local pottery at Cranberry Pottery, paintings and drawings at Gallery Tantalus, or leather crafts at Gurda Leather. On Texada Is. visit Harwood Point Park. Local celebrations include the Sea Fair — end July; Country Fair — end August; Folk Festival — beginning of September. The Powell River News is published Mondays and Wednesdays.

## Where To Stay And Eat:

Beach Gardens Resort Hotel — pool, tennis, boat charters, Sunset Room Restaurant with lounge and view: ☎ 485-6267; Westview Centre Motel: ☎ 485-4023, and others. Willingdon Beach Municipal Campground: ☎ 485-2242; Saltery Bay and Okeover Provincial Park Campgrounds. In Lund there is the Lund Breakwater Inn: ☎ 483-3187, or the Lund R.V. and Trailer Park (also campground): ☎ 483-4463. On Texada Island there is the Texada Arms Hotel: ☎ 486-7711, or Harwood Point Regional Campground: ☎ 486-7793. Dining Facilities at both the Texada Arms and the Breakwater.

**Visitor Information:** Powell River Chamber of Commerce, 6807 Wharf Street, Powell River, V8A 1T9.

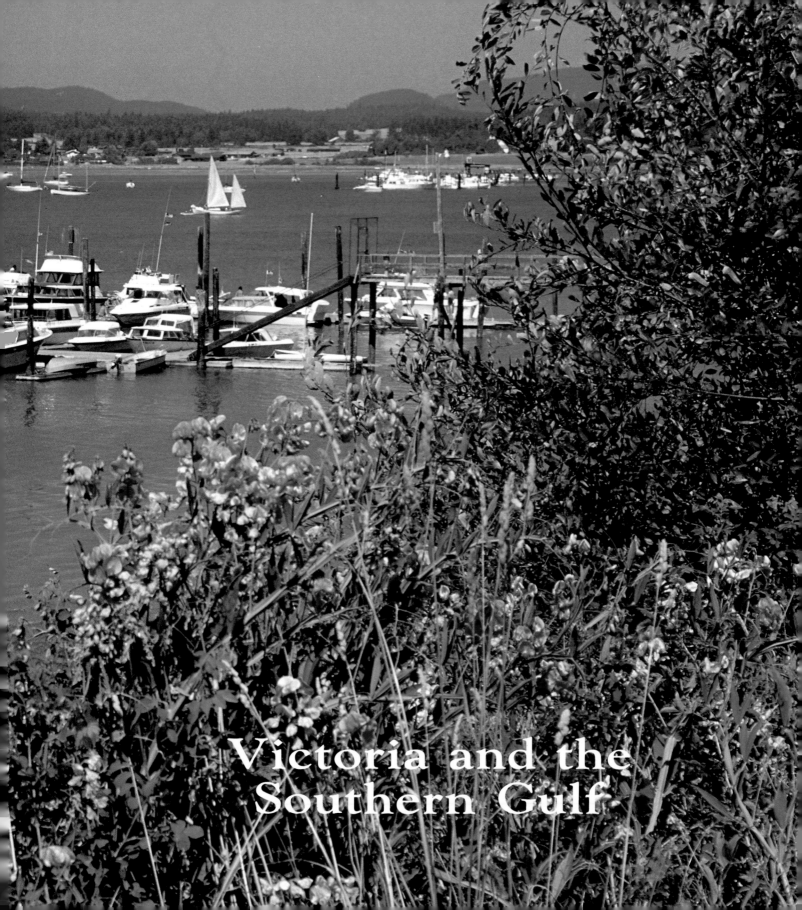

Victoria and the
Southern Gulf

*Victoria Inner Harbour:*
Stately ivy covered buildings, fine yachts, and the
sounds of the Carrilon, amid a profusion of
flowers.

*Victoria, The Old Town:*
Along the waterfront and through the narrow
alleys, buildings restored with pride.

*Chemainus, A Town Reborn:*
Even a deserted gas station is transformed to a
celebration of local history, as murals slowly
envelope even the town's way of life.

*Early Settlers Fence, Cowichan Valley.:*
The autumn joyfully culminates as leaves and soil merge again, preparing for next year's youthful bounty.

*Mayne Island, Georgina Point:*
Flowering meadows reach down to the shore. No
crowds, just the whisper of the sea.

*Saltspring Island, Beaver Point:*
The wind drops and last rays of the setting sun
turn the Gulf of Georgia to a sheet of beaten
bronze

# Victoria

*above:*
*A late, pale moon greets early-morning ferry riders.*

*left:*
*Downtown Victoria*
*Bright red London busses now augment the horse drawn Tally Ho to carry the visitor around the city sites decked with flowers.*

Gold! was the cry along the sand bars of the Fraser river and through the high plateaus of the Cariboo; gold was the lure that funneled twenty five thousand miners, speculators and entrepreneurs through the tiny Fort Victoria, a Hudson's Bay trading post, with a population of just three hundred. In just one year the Bastion town became the largest center of industry and commerce in the northwest and established Victoria as the local seat of government and its neighboring town of Esquimalt, with its deep water, as a strategic navy base. Today, the harsh frontier inhabitant has been replaced by a conservative tweedy and rather British Victorian in a capital city of British Columbia that conveys an atmosphere of a refined afternoon tea under soft light.

At the southernmost part of the province, sheltered from the vagueries of the blustering Pacific, Victoria enjoys a congenial temperate climate located between the Straits of Georgia Strait and Juan de Fuca; the Victoria region is not surprisingly a hub of both local and international ferry activity.

From the Inner harbour, right in the pulse of downtown Victoria, the Princess Marguerite leaves to cruises down Puget Sound to Seattle, the Black Ball ferries traverse Juan de Fuca's Strait to the magical Olympic Peninsula, snowy on the southern horizon. Commuter float planes provide rapid connections to the mainland and the northern Vancouver Island. All this from a harbour filled with fine yachts and where host is played to a spectrum of vessels and events like the Swiftsure and the Victoria — Maui Yacht Races, the harbour Festival and the Classic Boat Festival, which continue the cherishing of the classical floating world. A harbour bordered by magnificent buildings and throughout the seasons a riot of impeccably tended floral colour that spill from every available space. Victoria is an ideal city to explore on foot, while listening to the carillon sounds drifting off classic brick buildings. The ivy-covered Empress Hotel is an early railway hotel with a reputation to maintain for tea and crumpets, and lunch in the Bengall room. Along with the Parliament building it reigns over the Inner Harbour, from which just a few blocks away the restored and rejuvenated Old Town around Bastion Square, Market Square and Trounce Alley flourish with care and attention lavished on quaint shops, their brick and stone stripped of a hundred years of grime to proudly display their 19th century facades. Within, many still maintain an atmosphere of quiet old time commerce and through leaded glass windows visitors still see polite clerks serving across burnished wood and brass counters, showing their Scottish woolens, English bone china and Irish linens as if time here has stood still. But the Old Town has a modern flavor too with trendy boutiques and a host of fine international restaurants bordering the bricked pedestrian malls and open flower filled courts, while just a block away Chinatown starts with a whole new set of temptations for the pocketbook and the palate.

Victoria's traditional transportation, since the days of the Fort, of the horse drawn Tally Ho still runs but has now been augmented by bright red London busses making it easy for tourists to reach interesting spots away from the downtown centre. Everyone should see the Buchart Gardens; where once a gravel pit stood

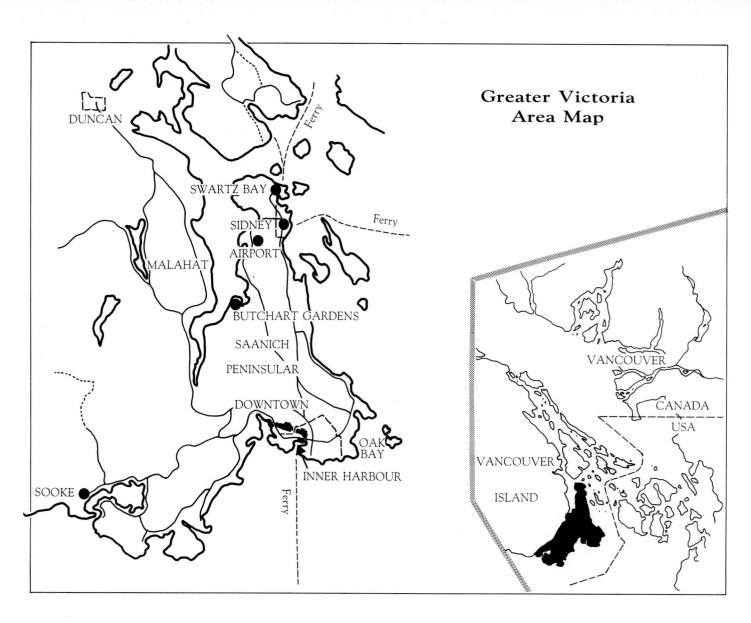

**Greater Victoria Area Map**

DUNCAN

Ferry

SWARTZ BAY

SIDNEY

Ferry

AIRPORT

MALAHAT

BUTCHART GARDENS

SAANICH

PENINSULAR

DOWNTOWN

OAK BAY

INNER HARBOUR

Ferry

SOOKE

VANCOUVER

CANADA

USA

VANCOUVER

ISLAND

a riot of colour now marks one of the world's most famous gardens, or travel along the winding shore where the green roll of the land looks too pastoral for a city setting; don't miss the incredible gardens in Oak Bay and Uplands.

To really see Victoria however a visitor should walk within the city. This is a city with a scale for walkers, a place to take one's time. Drop into the Provincial Museum, they offer history with a difference, an educational adventure of sights, sounds and stories that transport you through time itself. Browse the shops on Antique Row, feed the ducks and have a picnic under the gnarled Garry Oaks on Beacon Hill Park.

Do look over Robert Mackenzie's home, Craigflower Manor. Mackenzie was the colony's founder one hundred and thirty years ago. There are several structures from the early days still to be seen and well worth the visit. You will find Victoria is a city with a difference, it is a city on a scale for people, where a leisurely way of life, and some say eccentric as well, is not only maintained but is considered the most important aspect of the society.

Distant snowy summits and myriads of islands support the Victoria feeling of quiet celebrations. Parks and beaches abound, all within arm's reach, and wild flowers seep over the rolling knolls in the spring.

## How To Get There

**1. B.C. Ferries** Vancouver to Victoria Route; Sails from Tsawwassen (35km S. of Vancouver) to Swartz Bay (29km N.E. of Victoria. Sailing time – 1½hrs. See page 148 for phone nos. **2. Black Ball Ferry** Port Angeles (Washington) to Victoria – ☎ (604)386-2202(Victoria); or (206)457-4491(Port Angeles). **3. B.C. Steamship Company** (Princess Marguerite) Seattle to Victoria – Beginning of May to end of September – ☎ (604)386-1124(Victoria); or (206)682-8200 (Seattle). **4. Washington State Ferries** Anacortes (Wash) to Sidney (30km from Victoria) – ☎ 1-800-542 – 7052(Washington toll free); or 381-1551(Victoria). From northern Vancouver Island via Highways 19 and 1. **By Bus:** Pacific Coach Lines Vancouver to Victoria . Also serving all Vancouver Island – ☎ 683-9277(Vancouver);or 385-4411(Victoria); or listings at various way points. **By Train:** VIA Rail from Courtenay (mid-Vancouver Island) to Victoria and way points – ☎ 1-800-665-8630 toll free. **By Air:** Victoria International Airport at Sidney. Pacific Western Airlines from Vancouver – ☎ 684-6161; also Air Canada – ☎ 688-5515.

*above:*
*Beautiful parks are the settings for some of the finest of the carver's art.*

*left:*
*Picnic by the water with a backdrop of the Parliament Buildings.*

43

## How To Get Around

**Bus:** Metro Transit — ☎ 382-6161. Victoria Airporter — ☎ 388-9916. **Taxi:** Numerous, including Bluebird Cabs — ☎ 382-4235; Empress Taxi — ☎ 381-2222. Major car rentals at the airport or in town: Budget; Hertz; Sears; Tilden; etc. **City Tours:** A variety of sightseeing tours of the city and environs with The Gray Line — ☎ 388-9383. These tours leave at regular intervals from in front of the Empress Hotel. Or take a 1-hour tour on the horse-drawn Tallyho mid-May to end of September leaving every 20 minutes from beside the Parliament Buildings. **Bicycle Rental:** Island Sun Rentals (moped and bike) — ☎ 383-4424. **Boat Charter/Rental:** A random sampling — Harbour Charters — ☎ 384-1224; Langford Tool & Equipment Rentals, small boats and canoes — ☎ 478-6333; Victoria Sailing School, with or without sailing lessons — ☎ 384-7245 (Also offering 1-hour tours of the inner harbour in a Nootka Whaling Canoe); Ocean River Sports, ocean touring kayaks — ☎ 381-4233. Discovery Diving Adventures, diving excursions from Race Rocks to the Gulf Islands — ☎ 598-2124. **Horses:** Rockhaven Ranch — ☎ 478-3023. **Air Charter:** West Coast Air — ☎ 656-3971; Cougar Air Tours — ☎ 656-3968.

## Where To Stay And Eat

The venerable and prestigious Empress Hotel in the heart of the city is an institution for many tourists — ☎ 384-8111; however, within easy walking distance of the city centre Victoria boasts exceptional accommodation in a variety of price ranges. Listings are so numerous it may be wise to contact Reservations West computerized travel service and a confirmed accommodation booking in B.C. hotels, motels and resorts — ☎ 688-0044(Vancouver) or 1-800-663-1455 toll free. For those looking for the perfect *escape* to a secluded hideaway with superb cuisine, only 5 rooms, 30 min. from downtown Sooke Harbour House ☎ 642-3421. Another interesting alternative: Bed and Breakfast in private homes in the Victoria area: AAA Bed & Breakfast — ☎ 721-1234; or VIP Bed & Breakfast — ☎ 477-5604. Camping at three provincial parks: Goldstream, 15km N. of Victoria on Highway 1; French Beach, 35km W. of Victoria; or McDonald Park, 35km N.E.

**Restaurants:** Too numerous to attempt to list, exciting and initmate eateries throughout the Old Town, with a wide range of excellent cuisine. Consult Visitor's Information and local listings; one should not however miss afternoon tea at one of these three: The Empress, The Olde England Inn, or The Oak Bay Beach Hotel. You might also try a traditional Cantonese *dim sum* lunch in Chinatown.

Visitor Information: Greater Victoria Information Centre, 812 Wharf Street, Victoria, B.C. — ☎ 382-2127. This should be the first stopping point for all visitors to the city.

*Beautiful foreshore around the city is fringed by stands of the unusual Arbutus trees.*

## What To Do And See

Victoria was made for strolling and browsing. Begin by picking up brochures and advice at the Visitor's Information Centre on Wharf Street. Nearby you will find the Parliament Buildings (take a guided tour); the Provincial Museum (impressive exhibits of natural and human history, in particular the walk-in exhibits in the British Columbia Modern History section, plus an extensive collection of native Indian art); the Empress Hotel, *do stop for high tea in the lobby*, you will need reservations; the Undersea Gardens (underwater windows open onto prolific and fascinating sea life); the Royal London Wax Museum (lifesize replicas of royalty, famous and infamous people); Classic Car Museum; Miniature World (great moments in miniature, including the world's smallest operational sawmill); and the Crystal Gardens (glass enclosed tropical gardens and aviary, tea garden and boutiques). A little further north along the Inner Harbour is Chinatown with its "Gate of Harmonious Interest", and once notorious Fan Tan Alley. On the edge of Chinatown is the Harbour Public Market for fresh produce, fish, deli and international foods. Visit the Emily Carr Gallery on Wharf Street, or the artist's former home at the south end of Government St. The Victoria Art Gallery has a variety of exhibits; and also in the Rockland area is Government House, and Craigdarroch Castle built in the late 1800's and gradually being restored. Three heritage houses are open to the public: Helmcken House, Point Ellice House, and Craigflower Manor. Also interesting to tour is Anne Hathaway's Cottage and English Village with authentic 16th Century furnishings. Fable Cottage Estate offers fairy-tale architecture, colourful gardens, and an animated "Fantasy Forest".

Take a sightseeing trip along scenic Marine Drive to the world famous Butchart Gardens, a 35 acre floral showplace augmented by night illumination, summer theatre and fireworks displays. Along Marine Drive is Gyro Park at Cadboro Bay with its sandy beaches. Not far away is the University of Victoria campus. Closer to town Sealand offers underwater viewing, and trained seal, sea lion and killer whale shows. Close to city centre is the outstanding collection of totem poles at Thunderbird Park; and Beacon Hill Park with its lovely gardens, picnic and play areas, sports facilities

and zoo. The Dominion Astrophysical Observatory houses one of the world's largest reflecting telescopes along with astronomical displays; while the Maritime Museum at Bastion Square has a fine collection of historical marine items. Old Town shops stock a large variety of British goods — linens, woollens, and china. Bastion Square, Trounce Alley and Market Square are places to find interesting and unique boutiques and galleries, or browse the antique shops along Fort Street. Sample the many tea shops with their customary crumpets and scones.

A number of public and private golf courses include Glen Meadows — ☎ 656-3921; Gorge Vale — ☎ 386-3401; Cedar Hill Municipal Course — ☎ 595-2823. Tennis at Beacon Hill Park. Swimmingpools at Crystal Pool, Centennial Pool, or Oak Bay Recreation Centre. Warm water outdoor swimming at Beaver and Elk Lakes on the Saanich Peninsular. Live theatre at the Bastion or Belfry Theatres, or see what's current at the McPherson Playhouse. Local Celebrations include: Swiftsure Yacht Race — May; Oak Bay Tea Party — June; Highland Games — July.

*At low tide the remains of the old pier where early sailing ships once arrived.*

# Galiano and Mayne Islands

## Galiano Island

Galiano is a remarkably long and narrow island with a mountainous backbone of wooded summits. The island stretches itself between two of the most travelled passes in the Gulf Islands, to the North it dips down to Porlier Pass and to the South rising proudly at Active Pass.

Bluff Park stands 120 metres above Active Pass where fish boats and ferries tackle the surging currents below and above the bald eagles glide, their keen eyes searching the swirling waters for a worthy meal. Thousands of pink flowers drape the cliffsides in summer time and amid the panorama of the other islands, like scattered jigsaw pieces on all sides, the backdrop to the South of Mt.Baker sits like an unbelievable apparition. This is a place and a view with a thousand seasonal changes to draw visitors back and back and back once again.

Montague Harbour Provincial Park is situated in a protected bay with a beach, rocky spits and with mud flats filled with a selection of delicious clams, just waiting to be enjoyed.

## Mayne Island

The central location of Mayne has played a significant part through the island's past. Straining at the oars of their heavily laden skiffs, miners from Vancouver Island, on their way to the Fraser River Gold Rush found Mayne Island a good mid point in their travels to rest before tackling the black wirlpools of Active Pass. Miners Bay, as it came to be called, soon became a gathering spot for people waiting for mail and supplies to arrive by steamer and Mayne Island quickly became a focal point of transfer in the Islands, a position it still enjoys to this day in the inter-island ferry system. Mayne was for a while called *Little Hell* for all the pubs that it had in those early days and was chosen as the location for the only jailhouse on the Gulf Islands. Today, that compact jailhouse serves an appropriate function as the Mayne Museum.

Calm orchards and pastures seem distant from the raucous pioneer stories but *turn of the century* buildings like the Springwater Lodge still add more than a tinge of history to the island's atmosphere.

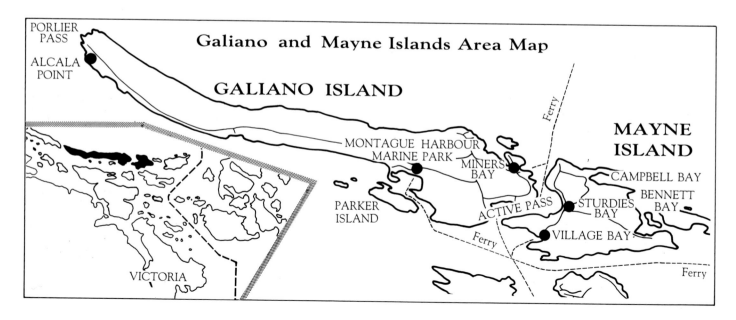

Galiano and Mayne Islands Area Map

*The bald eagles sway on the tree tops over the rushing waters in Active Pass.*

## What To Do And See

**Galiano Island:** Swim at the beautiful shell beach at Montague Park. Also beach access at Spotlight Cove, Ganner Rd., Georgeson Bay, Cain Dr., Twiss Rd. and Harper Rd. Hike to Bluffs Park view point overlooking Active Pass. View the spring wild flowers at Coon Bay (no picking, please) — You'll need a four-wheel drive. Bellhouse Park. **Hiking Trails:** Porlier Pass Drive to Pebble Beach or Cable Bay; Active Pass Road to Phillimore Point. **Shop** for local pottery at Earthen Things Gallery, and weaving and knitting at Small World gift shop. **Golf** at the Galiano Golf and Country Club (9 holes) ☎ 539-5533. **Mayne Island:** Beaches at Bennett Bay and Campbell Bay. View Active Pass lighthouse. The Plumper Pass *Lockup* is now a museum at Miner's Bay. Also built in the 1890's is the Church of St. Mary Magdalene. **Galleries:** for local arts include Mitchell Gallery, Artery, Charterhouse, Island Gallery, Root Seller, Studio Madrona. Visit the Mayne Island Producers' Market for produce and handcrafts each summer Saturday morning.

Consult the Gulf Islands *Driftwood* weekly newspaper, and especially the visitors' supplement for current activity listings.

## How To Get There

**By Car or Bicycle via B.C. Ferries: 1.** Vancouver Island to Outer Gulf Islands Route: Sails from Swartz Bay to Village Bay on Mayne Island, and to Montague Harbour on Galiano Island. **2.** Mainland to Gulf Islands Route: Sails from Tsawwassen to Village Bay on Mayne Island, and to Sturdies Bay on Galiano. Vehicle reservations are required on this route. (See page 148 for phone listings.) **By Bus to Major Ferry Terminals:** (See Saltspring Island) No bus transportation on the Gulf Islands.

**By Air:** Air B.C. to the Gulf Islands from Vancouver ☎ 685-3211, and Victoria ☎ 388-5151.

## How To Get Around

Your own car or bicycle is best. **Water Taxi:** Gulf Islands W.T. serves all of the Gulf Islands ☎ 537-2510 (Saltspring).**Galiano Island: Taxi and Water Taxi:** ☎ 539-2611. **Boat Charter:**Montague Charters; Box 26, Galiano Island, V0N 1P0. Gulf Islands Sailing Charter ☎ 539-2611. Galiano Landing Canoe Rental ☎ 539-2442. **Boat launching:** at Montague Harbour. **Horse Rental:** Bodega Farm ☎ 539-2677. **Mayne Island: Boat launching :**at Potato Point, David Cove and Piggot Bay.

## Where To Stay And Eat

**Galiano Island:** Galiano Lodge at the ferry landing ☎ 539-5252, Bodega Resort ☎ 539-2677, and others. Bed and Breakfast at The Berengerie ☎ 539-5392 and Holloway House ☎ 539-2581. Camping at Montague Provincial Marine Park. **Restaurants:** The Pink Geranium, a favourite among gourmands (You'll need a reservation) ☎ 539-2477; The Berengerie for a French flavour ☎ 539-5392; The Deli for take-outs; and the Humming Bird Inn pub. **Mayne Island:** Nineteenth Century surroundings at both Mayne Inn, 5km from Village Bay ☎ 539-2632, and Springwater Lodge at Miner's Bay ☎ 539-5521; and others. Bed and Breakfast at The Root Seller heritage house ☎ 539-2621, and Fernhill Herb Farm ☎ 539-2544. Restaurants at both the Mayne Inn and Springwater Lodge; also the Five Roosters at Miner's Bay.

# Pender and Saturna Islands

## The Pender Islands

Boat owners have always been attracted towards Pender Island. Located strategically on much travelled Boundary Pass, provided with it's two deep bays, Pender became a perfect place to refit for the scores of sailing vessels plying the Southern Gulf. In order to transport their provisioning goods easier and save an overland portage between Bedwell Harbour and Port Browning, in 1903 a 70 foot wide canal was dredged from Shark Cove over a narrow neck of land through to Bedwell and in so doing created the two Pender Islands that we have today. It was to be a further 52 years until local road transportation became important enough to reconnect the islands by a bridge over that same small boat passage.

North Pender is significantly the larger of these two hilly and wooded islands, however, still those same bays, almost surrounding South Pender, are a constant attraction to the many pleasure boats cruising the area and make a colourful flotilla display through the warm summer days.

To the appreciation of many visitors, public accesses to numerous beaches are well maintained and marked. Many of those beaches are embraced by small coves, so they tend to be quiet and secluded. Prior Centennial Provincial Park is well worth a leisurly visit, located between Hamilton and Medicine beaches, where campers can enjoy the quiet Gulf moods or where a simple picnic can become a long lasting memory.

Take the time to wind slowly through the older North Pender communities, *especially if you bring a bicycle*, of Port Browning, Port Washington, Otter Bay and Hope Bay. Here the houses, cabins and orchards are albums of long-time residence, although now by far, the largest proportion of residents live in the new community of Magic Lake Estates.

## Saturna Island

Saturna is an *outer* Gulf Island, at the southeast corner of the archipelago and thrusts out a long finger to the Canadian/U.S.A border at Boundary Pass. The island is mountainous, more remote and still rings with the sounds of logging high in the hills. Living on the island emphasizes independence and retreat for the very small population. With the big house at Boat Cove Lodge the only place of accommodation, and no public campgrounds, Saturna maintains a low tourism profile. However, the Provincial Park at Winter Cove encompasses long shorelines on both sides of Winter Point and provides beautiful shoreline walks where eagles can be seen patiently awaiting their lunch at the swirling waters of Boat Pass. East Point juts out abruptly, a bit like a renegade, to the lighthouse standing proudly on the tip and overlooking Boiling Reef, like an apostrophe of birds and sea life on the eroded sandstone.

Any languid pace of life is suspended around July 1 for the Saturna Island, Canada Day, Lamb Bake. Perhaps the biggest of annual Gulf Island events, the feast draws friends and visitors from afar.

## How To Get There

**By Car Or Bicycle via B.C. Ferries: 1.** Vancouver Island to Outer Gulf Islands Route: Sails from Swartz Bay to Otter Bay on Pender Island and to Saturna Island. **2.** Mainland to Gulf Islands Route: Sails from Tsawwassen to Otter Bay on Pender Island. Saturna passengers transfer at Mayne Island. Vehicle reservations are required on this route. By Bus to Major Ferry Terminals: No bus transportation on the Gulf Islands. *See page 121 for reservation phone listings and further details of connecting transportation services.*

**By Air:** Air B.C. to the Gulf Islands from Vancouver ☎ 685-3211, and Victoria ☎ 388-5151.

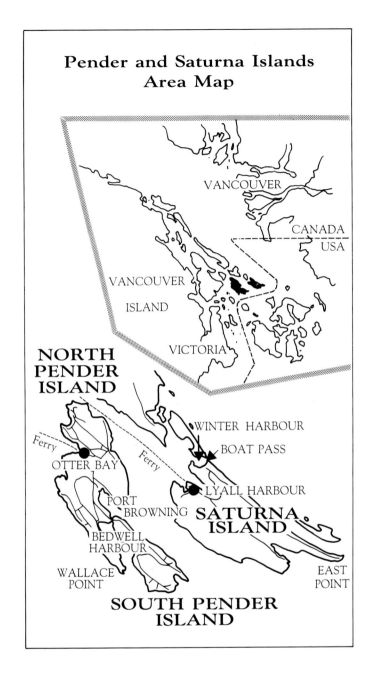

## Pender and Saturna Islands Area Map

VANCOUVER

CANADA
USA

VANCOUVER
ISLAND

VICTORIA

**NORTH
PENDER
ISLAND**

Ferry

OTTER BAY

Ferry

WINTER HARBOUR

BOAT PASS

LYALL HARBOUR

PORT
BROWNING

**SATURNA
ISLAND**

BEDWELL
HARBOUR

WALLACE
POINT

EAST
POINT

**SOUTH PENDER
ISLAND**

## How To Get Around

Your own car or bicycle is best. **Water Taxi:** Gulf Islands W.T. serves all the Gulf Islands ☎ 537-2510 (Saltspring). **Bicycle Rental:** Otter Bay Marina (Pender) ☎ 629-6301. **Boat Rental:** Bedwell Harbour Resort on South Pender ☎ 629-3212. **Boat Launching**-Pender: Browning Hb., and Otter Bay Marina. **Air Charter:** Harbour Air ☎ 122-800-0212(toll free).

## Where To Stay And Eat

**Pender Island:** Bedwell Harbour Resort (south); cottages/cabins ☎ 629-3212; Pender Lodge (north); close to Otter Bay, and well worth a visit, housekeeping cabins/rooms ☎ 629-3221; Port Browning Marina (north); cabins ☎ 629-3493. Cliffside Bed and Breakfast (north); also some tenting ☎ 629-6691. Camping at Prior Centennial Provincial Park and at Port Browning Marina. Wilderness walk-in camping at Beaumont Marine Park at Bedwell Harbour. Restaurants and licensed lounges at Pender Lodge and Bedwell Harbour Resort. Pubs at Bedwell Harbour Resort, and Browning Harbour. Deli and liquor store at Driftwood Centre near Browning Harbour.

**Saturna Island:** Accommodation at Boot Cove Lodge only ☎ 539-2254. No public campgrounds.

## What To Do And See

On **North Pender** beach access is off Armdale Rd., at Thieves Bay, at Wallace Point, and at Browning Harbour. Also access under the bridge between the islands (Good swimming here). On **South Pender** access is off Gowland Point Road. There are two pools, one at Bedwell Harbour and one at Browning Harbour. If you are not a guest at either resort then pay at the desk. Golfing is at Pender Island Golf and Country Club (9 holes) ☎ 629-6659. Tennis courts at Browning Harbour (at the school grounds on Canal Rd.), and at Pender Lodge. Shop for local pottery at The General Store, Hope Bay Store and Driftwood Centre.

**Saturna Island:** Very much off the beaten track. Lyall and Winter Harbours provide accessible beaches, or take in the view from Mt. Warburton Pike. At Winter Harbour take the short walk to Boat Pass and see the bald eagles keeping guard over the rushing torrent. Russell Beach is used for swimming and picnicking although it is private property. A favourite spot for salmon fishing is off East Point, where there are interesting weathered rocks to view the seals from and a good view of the lighthouse.

**Local Celebrations:** Saturna is famous for its lamb BBQ and fair held July 1 at Breezy Point. On Pender visit the Arts and Crafts Fair; Jul & Aug. Also the Fall Fair; end of Aug.

# The Cowichan Valley

The softly rolling land of the Cowichan and Chemainus valleys is broken by fences and scattered with farms that reflect the earliest times, when settlers, pushing north from Victoria, first found the rich soil and forest giants that have sustained the population through the years.

Along the shore, in a specially mild and sunny climate, the bright naked orange Arbutus trunks lean out over eroded sandstone rocks, worn by the cold surging waters as the tides rush through the offshore Gulf Islands.

The early days were not always tranquil. Settlers competed for nature's spoils with a particularly warrior-like native peoples often resulting in the bringing in of military firepower to force the issue. Today the native peoples of the Cowichan Valley are world reknowned for their unique wool; spun, knitted and woven in their traditional ways, with sea monsters and birds of the imagination.

Today, with the forest industry becoming more a part of history than a future for the area, the town of Chemainus has shown people's remarkable resilience by becoming an exciting centre for the arts. Large murals resonate from walls throughout the town, quite ordinary buildings are transformed to make magical stage sets for daily life, depicting the past of the valley and its maritime connection. In that same vein of heritage recognition is the construction, just a few blocks from downtown, of a nineteenth century brigantine replica, like the tall ships that once carried lumber from Chemainus throughout the world. Each year as more mural scenes are added around the town the artistic endeavours draws to the area even more talent and more drive to give further deserved pride to the population in their living celebration of the area's history.

Thetis Island has long been well-known to boaters because of it's protected and attractive bay at Telegraph Harbour where the marinas tempt yachters

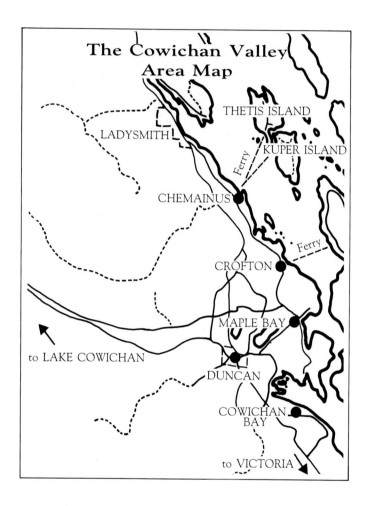

The Cowichan Valley Area Map

and landlubbers alike with home-style cooking and local crafts such as the cozy Cowichan sweaters. The narrow channel between Thetis and Kuper Islands is so shallow that it dries at low water, rocky and shell covered for beachcombers of all ages.

Once known and feared for it's ferocious inhabitants, Kuper Island is almost entirely Cowichan Indian reservation land. One hundred acres of farmland, called Folded Hills, once belonged to a Christian organization. Receiving few visitors, and little development, Kuper Island today is calm and peaceful and seems to remain apart from time.

*Petroglyphs carved into the soft sandstone are part of our unrecorded past*

## What To Do And See

### Chemainus/Crofton:

Hike from Osborne Bay Park to Maple Mountain Park viewpoint. See the Chemainus Historical Murals and watch new ones in the making at the July Festival of Murals. Watch the construction of the Brigantine, "Spirit of Chemainus". Waterwheel Park, Locomotive Park, and the Chemainus water Wheel are worth a visit, as is the Crofton Museum on Emily Street. Take the Chemainus ferry to Saltspring Island for fishing, swimming and hiking. Golf at Mount Brenton Golf Course ☎ 246-9322. Shop for works by west coast artists and artisans at Great West Art, Chemainus; local rhodonite carvings, jasper beads at George Jewellers, Chemainus. You may have to travel 15km south to Duncan for the best selection of Cowichan Indian sweaters. Local Celebrations: Kinsmen Fun Daze; Crofton Salmon BBQ – July.

## How To Get There

**By Car or Bicycle: 1.** From Horseshoe Bay (Vancouver) via B.C. Ferries to Nanaimo (1½hrs) then south. **2.** From Tsawwassen (Vancouver) via B.C. Ferries to Victoria, then north on Highway 1 toward Nanaimo. **3.** Highway 19 south from Port Hardy, or Comox/Courtenay.

### Chemainus and Crofton:

**By Car:** Chemainus and Crofton are 35 to 40km south of Nanaimo on Highway 1. **By Bus:** Pacific Coach Lines (See Nanaimo). **By Train:** via Rail (See Nanaimo). **By Air:** Air B.C. from Vancouver ☎ 685-3211, or Victoria ☎ 388-5151 to Cassidy Airport, 20km north of Chemainus.

### Thetis and Kuper Island:

Thetis and Kuper Islands are reached via Ministry of Highways ferry service from Chemainus. ☎ (Victoria)387-3053.

## How To Get Around

### Chemainus/Crofton:

**Car Rental;** Budget Rent-A-Car ☎ 748-3221(Duncan). **Local Bus Service:** McBride's Service Station – ☎ 246-3341. **Taxi:** Crofton Taxi ☎ 246-3023; Chemainus Taxi – ☎ 246-4774. **Boat Rental/Charter:** G. & L. Charters ☎ 246-4059; Bluenose Marina (Cowichan Bay) ☎ 748-2222; Cove Yachts (Maple Bay), sailing charters ☎ 748-8136. **Boat Launching:** Kin Beach (Chemainus); Crofton ferry terminal. **Air Charter:** Burrard Air (Cassidy Airport) ☎ 245-4833.

### Thetis and Kuper Island:

On both islands it is best to have one's own car or bike for transportation.

## Where To Stay And Eat

### Crofton/Chemainus:

Twin Gables Resort Motel (Crofton) ☎ 246-3112; Fuller Lake Chemainus Motel ☎ 246-3282; Country Maples Campground ☎ 246-2078. Cowichan Valley Bed and Breakfast, choice of locations – Call Peter Milner at 743-3386. The Brass Bell (Crofton) for seafood; Willow Street Teahouse; Mom's Kitchen for home cooked meals; Saltair Pub – 3km north of Chemainus in an old restored house.

### Thetis Island

Overbury Farm Resort ☎ 246-9769; or the Marina for seafood.

## How To Get There

**By Car or Bicycle:** Washington State Ferries; Sidney (Vancouver Island) to San Juan Islands, or Anacortes (Washington State) to San Juan Islands. ☎ 1-800-542-7052 (Washington toll free) or (604)381-1551 (Victoria). Customs and immigration at Sidney and Anacortes.

**By Air:** San Juan Airlines from Seattle/Tacoma and Bellingham. In Washington State ☎ (800)438-3880, outside Washington ☎ (206)452-1323. Lake Union Air Service; seaplane from Seattle to San Juan ☎ (206)284-2784 collect.

## Where To Stay And Eat

**San Juan Island:** Friday Hbr Motor Inn ☎ 378-4351; Roche Hbr Resort ☎ 378-2155. Bed and Breakfast at Collins House, Friday Hbr ☎ 378-5834; or Tucker House, Friday Hbr ☎ 378-2783. Camping at Lakedale Campground, and San Juan County Park. Numerous eateries including The Gollywobbler for home cooking; Electric Company tavern featuring weekend jazz; Cannery House, a lunch hotspot; Bacchus Carry-out Cuisine for gourmets; and many more.

**Orcas Island:** Deer Harbour Marina & Resort ☎ 376-4420; Rosario Resort, Eastsound ☎ 376-2222. Bed and Breakfast at Kangaroo House, Eastsound ☎ 376-2175; or Woodsong, Westsound ☎ 376-2340. Camping at Moran State Park ☎ 376-2326. A number of restaurants including Bilbos, popular for seafood & Spanish dishes; the Bungalow with jazz in the lounge, Dickie's Deli in the Eastsound market.

**Lopez Island:** The Islander Lopez, resort, hotel & marina, Fisherman's Bay ☎ 468-2233. Bed and Breakfast at Betty's Place (island north) ☎ 468-2506; or Aleck Bay Inn (island south) ☎ 468-2506. Hummel Haven Bicycle Camp, Centre Rd. for hikers & bikers ☎ 468-2217.

**Telephone:** The area code to the U.S. Islands is 206 from B.C.. Dial 1-206-then the local number; from Washington dial 1 followed by the local number. The area code to the Canadian Islands is 604. From B.C. dial 1-followed by the local number; from Washington dial 1-604-local number.

## How To Get Around

**By Bus:** San Juan Tours & Transit; regular runs from Friday Harbour to Roche Harbour Resort. **Taxi Cab** (San Juan Island only): Taxi San Juan ☎ 378-4711. **Car Rental:** San Juan Car Rentals – pickup and delivery locations throughout the islands. **Bicycle Rental:** Island Bicycles, Friday Harbour – free maps and advice; Roche Harbour Resort (summer); Island Chain Saw, Eastsound. On Orcas Island: San Juan Bicycle Works, Lopez Plaza; Islander Lopez Resort. **Moped Rental:** San Juan Scooters, Friday Hbr; Roche Hbr Resort; Friday Hbr Motor Inn; Key Moped Rentals, Eastsound, Orcas; Islander Lopez Resort. **Boat Charter/Rental:** San Juan Charters (power and sail) ☎ 378-5390; Black Bottom Boats, Eastsound, Orcas ☎ 376-4032; Islands Marine Centre, Fisherman's Bay, Lopez ☎ 468-2279; and numerous others. Also in Moran State Park. **Canoe Rental:** at the fuel dock at Roche Harbour. **Air Charter:** Island Air Express ☎ (206)378-5375; West Isle Air ☎ (206)293-4691. **Horse Rental:** Spoon River Ranch near Roche Harbour; The Equestrian Castle near the Orcas ferry landing.

*Old wooden structures are receptive to the cool breeze coming off the water*

*A boaters's paradise in quiet, secluded waters.*

## What To Do And See

**San Juan Island:** San Juan Island National Historic Park in two locations: the English Camp, 16km NW of Friday Hbr; and the American Camp, 8km SE of Friday Hbr — explore the old buildings and ruins, picnic, hike the trails & beaches or take a scheduled nature walk. South Beach, near the American Camp, is the longest public beach, and offers scheduled tide pool excursions (in season). Take a walking tour of the historic buildings at Roche Harbor. Visit the Ocean Research Station at the Friday Harbor Marine Laboratories ☎ 378-2165 for appointment. Also at Friday Hbr, the Whale Museum and the San Juan Historical Museum. San Juan Kayak Expeditions offer 2,3 and 4-day excursions ☎ 378-4436. Visit and shop the many galleries offering the work of local artists; Granny Quacker's Nest, Island's Own, The Sandpebble, Sunshine Gallery, and more.

**Tourist Information:** San Juan Island Chamber of Commerce, 450 Spring Street West, Friday Harbour, WA 98250.

**Orcas Island:** Moran State Park for hiking trails, lake fishing, swimming, and the spectacular view from Mt. Constitution. See the impressive collection of pioneer artifacts and Indian art at the Orcas Island Museum in Eastsound. Island galleries include Eagle View Leatherworks at the ferry landing; Darvill's Rare Print Shop, Otter's Lair Pottery, or The Mythical Beast in Eastsound. A potpourri of crafts are offered at The Orcas Island Artworks in Olga.

**Lopez Island:** Spencer Spit State Park for camping, trail and beaches. Also Odlin Park & Hummel Haven Bicycle Camp on Hummel Lake. Hike and explore the environment at Shark Reef. Island historical displays and a marine exhibit are housed at Lopez Island Museum in Lopez Village.

The islands make for great cycling, and there is golfing on all three. Biggest event of the year is the San Juan Jazz Festival held at the end of July; book your accommodations well in advance.

Consult *The Journal of the San Juan Islands* (weekly), especially the Springtide issue, for a complete visitors' guide.

# The Hub of Vancouver Island

*Bamfield, Liz Happynook:*
For Liz, who's baskets are in heavy demand, much time in the summer is spent sorting the grasses to be used for weaving through the following winter.

*Hornby Island, Heinz Laffin:*
There is a peace in Heinz's studio, like the
smoothness of his pottery shapes.

*Qualicum Falls:*
The deep cool gorge, brimmed with flowers amid
the evergreens, trimmed with mosses and alive
with the sounds of water.

*Long Beach:*
A beach, wide and white, that seems to go
forever..

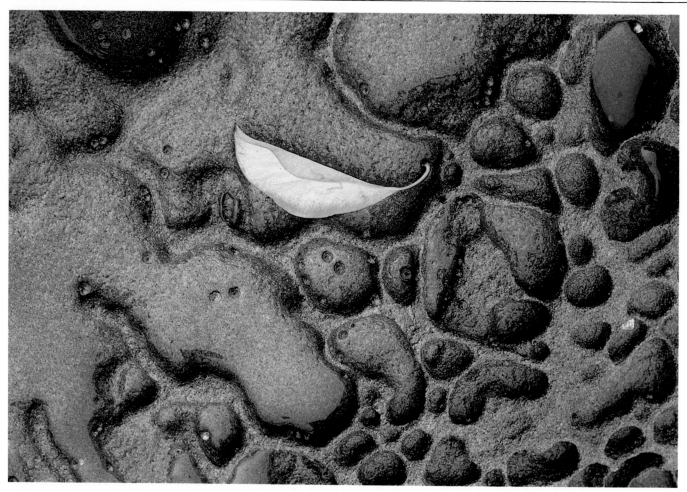

*Arbutus Leaf:*
The Arbutus are special to our weathered
sandstone shores, they speak of warm balmy
summer days, and Sea Otters playing tag among
the kelp floats.

*Hornby Island, Sammy Sammy:*
A legend on the island, Sammy Sammy gives a ghost show with his puppets to tell one of his *life* stories.

*Touquart Bay, Barkley Sound:*
A bridge designed for thundering trucks now gives
easy access to the calm waters deep within the
sound.

*Combers Beach:*
Driven high by the pounding Pacific, logs, enough
to build a kingdom, are strewn along the shore.

*Long Beach:*
Small islands are beached by the prodigious tides and glassy pools provide an insight into nature to stun the imagination.

*Broken Group Islands:*
White shell beaches, crystal clear water, solitude;
only the raucus raven keeps us company.

*Hornby Island:*
The trollers are in for the night, the wind has
dropped and silence fills the evening.

*Gabriola Island:*
The pines along the bluff, twisted by the winds,
are barely moving now in the last light.

# Nanaimo

Bath tubs, like a great swarm of enraged hornets, engines screaming, swarm off from the calm of Nanaimo's harbour in the World Championship Race, to face the open Georgia Strait and finish in Vancouver during the July Sea Festival. Fortunately, a drier form of crossing of the Strait between the two cities is provided by B.C. Ferries, making Nanaimo a major gateway and hub for visitors to Vancouver Island; appropriately, even the native name for this important city of *sne-ny-mo*, meaning *a meeting place*.

Nanaimo, once a major Hudson Bay fort and trading centre, is now a busy port, mainly dependant on forest products and fishing although in earlier times was the focal point of a large coal mining area where old mining shafts extend below the waters of the Strait to Newcastle Island and beyond. The older part of town and the reconditioned 'blockhouse' sits above the waterfront where newly developed parkland provide leisure opportunities centrally located for the community and visitors.

Newcastle Island Marine Park and the adjacent residential Protection Island are just a few minutes away from downtown and reached from the Queen Elizabeth II Promenade by the little red-trimmed ferry Arabella carying 55 people on a music-accompanied passage. Idyllic Newcastle Island is a blend of woods, meadows and beaches providing a portrait of historic development, with sites of an Indian village, a sandstone mill grinder quarry, a coal mine, a herring saltery and the Canadian Pacific Railway resort pavilion.

## Gabriola Island

Gabriola Island, just 25 minutes by ferry from downtown Nanaimo, sandwiched between the lights of Nanaimo and Vancouver, remains a rural island of tranquillity. The approach from the ferry presents a screen of weathered sandstone cliffs formed to fluid-like bulges, swerves and overhangs is a popular attraction at Malaspina Galleries. Historically significant Indian petroglyphs are to be found on the island.

Gabriola Sands Provincial Park is on a spoon-shaped peninsula with beaches on both sides of the spoon handle. It looks toward the coast range across Georgia Strait.

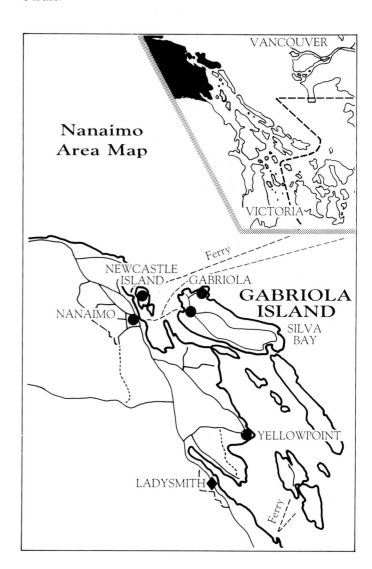

**Nanaimo Area Map**

## Visitor Information:

Nanaimo Tourist Bureau, 100 Cameron Rd., V9R 2X1.

## How To Get There

### Nanaimo:

**By Car or Bicycle: 1.** From Horseshoe Bay (Vancouver) via B.C. Ferries to Nanaimo (1½hrs). **2.** From Tsawwassen (Vancouver) via B.C. Ferries to Victoria, then north on Highway 1 to Nanaimo (112km). **3.** Highway 19 south from Port Hardy (389km), or Comox/Courtenay (108km).

### Gabriola Island:

**By Car or Bicycle:** Ministry of Highways ferry from Nanaimo (20 min). **By Bus:** Pacific Coach Lines to Nanaimo from Vancouver, Victoria and Vancouver Island way-points ☎ 385-4411(Victoria), or ☎ 280-9439(Vancouver). **By Train:** via Rail to Nanaimo from Victoria or Courtenay and Vancouver Island way-points ☎ 1-800-665-8630(toll free). **By Air:** Air B.C. ☎ 388-5151(Victoria), or 685-3211(Vancouver); Harbour Air ☎ 1-800-0212(toll free).

## What To Do And See

### Nanaimo:

Bowen Park contains a recreation centre, picnic sites, and wooded trails along the Millstream. Newcastle Island Provincial Park — a 10-minute passenger ferry ride from Nanaimo — offers delightful areas for swimming, beachcombing, picnicking and walking trails. Scuba, sailing, and fishing are popular. Take a walking tour of the city centre and Princess Royal Promenade, or try one of the bicycle routes. Visit the Bastion, a historic old Hudson's Bay fort, now a museum. A miner's cottage and other coal mining relics are to be found at Piper Park, along with the Centennial Museum and its display of pioneer artifacts including a replica of a coal mining shaft. Just south of the city is Petroglyph Park with its ancient Indian rock carvings. Admire the panoramic view from Malaspina College, visit the Japanese Garden and Natural History Museum. Golf at the Nanaimo Golf and Country Club ☎ 758-6332. Swimming at Departure Bay, Newcastle Avenue Beach, Piper's Lagoon; or Nanaimo River, Westwood or Long Lakes.Tennis courts and swimming pool at Bowen Park.

**Local Celebrations:** Empire Days — end May; World Bathtub Race — July; Island Exhibition — Aug.

### Gabriola:

Sandy beaches for swimming, picnicking at Gabriola Sands Provincial Park, or walks along Drumbeg Beach. The Malaspina Galleries are spectacular rock formations made for photographing. Try fishing, or gather shellfish. Beach access is at Taylor Bay and Whalebone Beach. Tennis courts are at Silva Bay and Surf Lodge Resorts. Local pottery is found at Silva Bay Marina, Sunstone Pottery at Pilot Bay, or Ye Old Beanery Restaurant at the ferry.

## How To Get Around

### Nanaimo:

**Regional Transit** ☎ 390-4111. **Taxis:** several including A.C. Taxi ☎ 753-1231; Airporter ☎ 754-4631. **Car Rental:** several including Hertz ☎ 754-1381; Budget ☎ 753-1195. **Boat Rental/Charter:** Brechin Point Marina ☎ 753-6122, and others. **Boat Launching:** Brechin Point, and Piper's Lagoon. **Scuba Rental:** Seafun Divers ☎ 754-4813. **Windsurfers:** Kona Buds ☎ 758-2911. **Bicycle Rental:** Peddle Pusher Bike Shop — ☎ 753-5555; Hank's Bicycle Shop ☎ 754-6221. **Riding:** M & M Stables ☎ 753-3885. **Air Charter:** Air B.C. ☎ 753-3494; Burrard Air ☎ 753-6541.

### Gabriola:

*Own car or bike is best.* **Taxi:** Gabriola Cabs ☎ 247-9348. **Boat Rental/Charter:** Silva Bay Resort ☎ 247-9267. **Boat Launching:** Silva Bay, and Degnen Bay.

## Where To Stay And Eat

### Nanaimo:

Tally Ho Town and Country Inn, central ☎ 754-2241; Inn of the Sea, 18km south ☎ 245-2211; Moby Dick Boatel ☎ 753-7111; Yellowpoint Lodge located 20km SE is a now famous retreat for many who return year after year for the rustic charm and quiet overlooking the Gulf ☎ 245-7422, and others. Ivy Green Provincial Campground, and Newcastle Island Provincial Park (camping). For dining: The Grotto ☎ 753-3303; Chez Michel ☎ 754-1218; Tio's ☎ 754-4812 — all with views. And numerous others.

### Gabriola:

Haven By the Sea Resort ☎ 247-9211; Surf Lodge ☎ 247-9231; Silva Bay Resort ☎ 247-9267.

# Parksville and Qualicum

There is always a sense of holiday and established stability along the wide safe beaches and through the cool parklands that brings many visitors to the Qualicum Beach and Parksville coast line time and again for their summer vacations; here, a sense of family is felt and a leisurely pace is the established way of life. The deck chair, stack of books and barbecue are important tools in this land, as are the bucket and spade for the youngsters. The gentle sands and wide ranging tides encourage kids of all ages to dig for the evening clam pot, while protected waters, close to the salmon spawning rivers, bring out anglers in boats of every shape and size from first-light until dark.

But behind those shores there are other worlds, very different and very striking; a world of deep gorges and misting waterfalls and the world of deep emerald green, with trees and forests beyond compare. Two parks, the Englishman River Falls and the Little Qualicum Falls, both make a quiet haven away from the crowds where the sensuous skinned Arbutus tree stands alongside, and is dwarfed by, the giant Douglas Fir; rainbows grow right out of the thundering rocky canyons to deliciously cool us in their sweeping spray. A few kilometers away at the MacMillan Park the virgin timber stands, humbling us with its stature, inconceivably tall, and, providing in the deep forest recesses, just a brief glimpse of this coast and nature as it was before the white man and modern industry arrived.

This corner of the coast-line accommodates a wide range of visitors with unassuming ease. The range of hotels and motels is prodigious and excellent food can be found to satisfy even the most jaded palate.

Lasqueti, more visited by boaters than by ferry riders, is an island of seclusion, reached by a passenger-only ferry from French Creek to the village of False Bay. Roads on the island are not paved and the residents of Lasqueti have elected not to have electric power supplied. The feeling on Lasqueti is of living both close to the land and sea. Houses have personality, thronged by vegetable gardens and walkways of broken shells. The sense of communal ease shows through the friendly waves from the children ambling down the road. A stone mansion with two chimneys tells an entertaining tale. Back in the 1920's, if smoke was coming out of the chimney shaped like a teapot, it signalled that moonshine whiskey was on the market. The Teapot House is now a restaurant with fresh creative food and a very pleasant ambience sometimes enhanced with live music.

## How To Get There

By Car: Parksville and Qualicum are north of Nanaimo 37km and 48km respectively along Highway 19. **By Bus:** Pacific Coach Lines (See Nanaimo). **By Train:** via Rail (See Nanaimo). **By Air:** Aquila Air Ltd. ☎ 752-6511(Qualicum).

### Lasqueti Island:

The Ministry of Highways operate a small ferry from French Creek, 6 km. north of Parksville. No cars. Sailings are infrequent and visitors should check the current schedule. ☎ (Victoria)387-3053.

## How To Get Around

Taxi ☎ 248-5741. **Boat Rental/Charter:** Beachcomber Marina ☎ 468-7222, Schooner Cove Resort ☎ 468-7691, both located at Nanoose Bay, 12km south of Parksville, and both with boat launching. **Boat Launching:** At Government boat basin at French Creek, and at Qualicum Beach. **Air Charter:** Aquila Air Ltd. ☎ 752-6511.

### Lasqueti:

Your own **bicycle**. Enquire at the store for taxi service.

## Where To Stay And Eat

Island Hall Resort Hotel in Parksville ☎ 248-3225 (or Vancouver 681-3800); Qualicum College Inn ☎ 752-9262; plus a number of motels, campgrounds and trailer parks. Provincial Government campground at Rathtrevor Beach. Go out of your way to enjoy the superb French cuisine at Ma Maison in Parksville ☎ 248-5859; or for old charm, The Judges Manor ☎ 248-2544. In Qualicum, the College Inn for elegant dining, or the Tudor Tearooms for a English tea.

### Lasqueti:

No accommodation. There is a cafe at the ferry dock, or try charming Teapot House ☎ 333-8805.

**Visitor Information:** Parksville, Qualicum and Lasquiti Island Chamber of Commerce, P.O. Box 99, V0R 2S0.

## What To Do And See

Miles of sandy beaches for swimming and beachcombing. Inland, Englishman River Falls with wooded trails waterfalls and petroglyphs; and Little Qualicum Falls are impressive. Visit Cathedral Grove, to see one of the last stands of virgin Douglas Fir, in MacMillan Park. For the more adventurous (and knowledgable) there are the Horne Lake Caves. The Big Qualicum River Fish Hatchery offers a fascinating way to learn about our local salmon and trout. On Highway 4A just west of Qualicum, visit the Hamilton Swamp Trail and Bird Sanctuary; or the Canadiana Museum on Highway 19 with its collection of Inuit and pioneer artifacts. Saltwater and freshwater fishing abound. Golf at Qualicum Beach Golf Club ☎ 752-6312, or Eaglecrest Golf and Country Club ☎ 752-6311. Local celebrations include Parksville Pageant Days – July; the Coombs Country Festival – May and Aug.

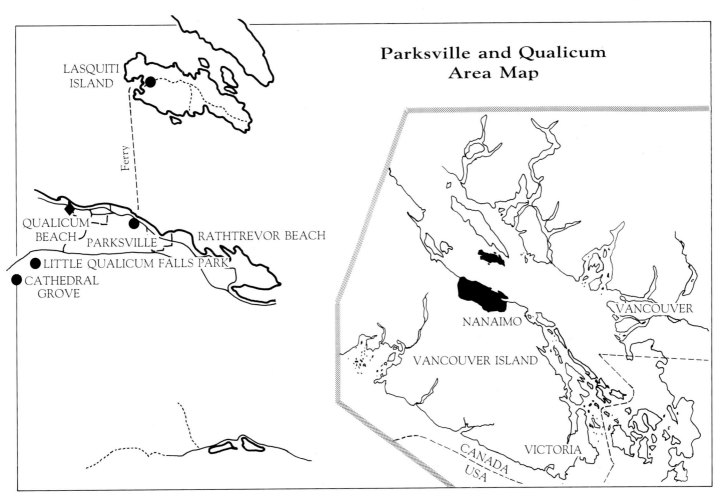

**Parksville and Qualicum Area Map**

LASQUITI ISLAND

Ferry

QUALICUM BEACH

PARKSVILLE

RATHTREVOR BEACH

LITTLE QUALICUM FALLS PARK

CATHEDRAL GROVE

NANAIMO

VANCOUVER

VANCOUVER ISLAND

VICTORIA

CANADA
USA

# Denman And Hornby Islands

The separation of Denman and Hornby from the mainland by just a narrow channel of Baynes Sound water has created in the population a rugged self-sufficient style of life that has attracted a broad range of artists and crafts-people to these rustic islands.

Denman today is a placid land of classic old churches and farm houses, where it is difficult to believe that at the beginning of the century there were three logging railroads on this island that is only 20 km long and only 6 km at it's widest part. Denman however has always been a farming community and throughout the island weathered barns and fine old farmhouses bring a wonderful character to the land. The General Store and Cafe is a comfortable place that could adequately symbolize the relaxed pace of island country living, while neighbouring the store are the Denman Crafts cabin, the museum and a rambling community hall. The coastline has small coves and beaches interspersed with steep wooded slopes. At the northern tip Henry Bay has a fine sandy beach, or try just south of the ferry landing at Metcalf Bay for another. At the southern tip of the island the high sea cliffs and rock pinnacles crowd the shore with giant boulders and an open panorama to the southern waters.

Hornby Island rises steeply to the west where the ferry slides in close under the abrupt slopes of Mount Geoffrey and cool winding and wooded road lead visitors across an island dotted with long established farms, to where at Tribune and Whaling Station Bays wide sandy beaches provide a place for quiet relaxation. Sculpted in the sandstone Indian petroglyphs border Heron Rocks and Ford's Cove and spring flowers crown the bluffs at Helliwell Park at the far eastern island tip.

The Island draws many summer visitors with a wide range of diverse attractions. People gather around the crafts displays and tempting foods at the Co-op store.

*The now old-fashioned general store brings character to this town.*

In the evenings there are events like the Shoestring Operas, the Chamber Music Society's concerts, and Sammy Sammy's ghost show for children. For the more adventurous, the appearances of six-gill sharks at local dive spots draw the scuba diver.

The Community Hall is a unique structure built by the efforts of the islanders, as was the school. They are true examples of the co-operation between people who choose where they live and are very concerned with their quality of life.

## Denman And Hornby Islands Area Map

VANCOUVER

ISLAND

NANAIMO

LONGBECK
POINT

CHICKADEE
LAKE

**DENMAN**

Ferry

BUCKLEY
BAY

FILLONGLEY
PROVINCIAL
PARK

**ISLAND**

BAYNES

SOUND

GRAVELLY
BAY

**HORNBY
ISLAND**

Mt.
GEOFFREY

HELLIWEL
PROVINCIAL
PARK

TRIBUNE
BAY

## How To get There.

**By car or bicycle:** Department of Highways ferry from Buckley Bay (Vancouver Island) to Denman Island (15min.), then a 10min. drive across Denman Island to the Department of Highways ferry to Hornby Island(15min.) **By Bus:** Pacific Coach Lines from Vancouver, Victoria and Island way points to Buckley Bay ☎ 385-4411 (Victoria), or 280-9439 (Vancouver.) **By Rail:** VIA Rail from Victoria and way points ☎ 1-800-665-8630 (toll free.) **By Air:** Air B.C. from Victoria ☎ 388-5151, or Vancouver 685-3211. Aquila Air Hornby Island to Qualicum (Vancouver Island) with Vancouver connections ☎ 752-6511 (Qualicum)

## How To Get Around.

Best by private car or bicycle. **Boat rental/charter:** On Hornby – Fords Cove Marina for rentals and also charter yacht ☎ 335-0721. On Denman – Baynes Sound Fishing Charters ☎ 335-2615. **Boat launch:** Hornby – The Thatch. Denman – Bayne Sound ferry dock and Gravelly Bay. Diving packages at Hornby Island Diving.

## Where To Stay And Eat.

**Hornby:** The Thatch Restaurant, Pub and Campsite ☎ 335-0136 (Also, groceries are available at Rosemary's Corner Store at The Thatch.) Sea Breeze Lodge ☎ 335-2321; Woodlane Bed and Breakfast ☎ 335-2208; Trin Bay House Rental (weekly) ☎ 339-5181; Fords Cove Marina, Cottages and Campground ☎ 335-2169 (also groceries); Sandpiper Ridge Lodge ☎ 335-2771; Bradsdadsland Campground ☎ 335-0757. **Denman:** Denman Island Guest House and Restaurant ☎ 335-2688; Tait's Bed and Breakfast ☎ 335-2640; Sea Canary B and B- ☎ 335-2949; Lakefront Campsites ☎ 335-2368; Ocean Park Campground ☎ 335-0860; Fillongley Provincial Park on the east side of the island. Denman Island Store and Cafe.

## What To Do And See.

The islands are great for cycling, hiking, swimming, diving, and beachcombing. Stroll through Fillongley Park on Denman, enjoy the beach, or take the hiking trails to Chikadee Lake or Longbeck Point. Visit the Denman Museum. On Hornby, swim at Tribune Bay's beautiful beach or explore Helliwell Provincial Park. Hike to 1000ft. Mt. Geoffrey. Visit the petroglyphs at Whaling Station Bay and Fords Cove. Shop for some of the local craft work sold directly from cottage workshops such as Anvil Studios for custom Designs in precious metals- ☎ 335-2751: Earthen Vessels for pottery ☎ 335-2430; or Romantics for custom silk designs and lingerie ☎ 335-2714 – all on Hornby. Or Cedar Ship Woodcraft ☎ 335-2415; Le Baron Pottery ☎ 335-0198 – both on Denman. The Thatch on Hornby, and Denman Crafts on Denman also carry work by local artisans.

**Tourist Information:** Denman Island Store, or Hornby- Denman Tourist Association, c/o Brian Bishop, Hornby Island, B.C. V0R 1Z0 ☎ 335-2321

# Barkley Sound to Long Beach

Untamed, with pounding surf and calm twinkling islands, lush mossy rain forests and white sandy beaches as far as the eye can see, the west coast of Vancouver Island and particularly the Barkley Sound area, lures visitors from all over the world. This is a primitive unpopulated and unspoiled piece of coastline that provides an opportunity to experience a new nature, so beautiful that our very idea of nature may be changed forever.

At the tip of the octopus arm of Alberni Inlet, closer to Vancouver Island's east coast than the west, Port Alberni sits, a shipping harbour, a fishing centre, hub of the island's forest resources and backdropped by the rocky peak of Mt. Arrowsmith. The town is a way point for those who travel down the winding inlet by boat or the equally winding road deep between the snow-capped mountains and following the shimmering water out to the west.

Black and white, the staunch freighter Lady Rose sails out of Alberni Canal to the islands and inlets of Barkley Sound, calling in at tiny logging communities, carrying passengers, cargo and mail. A brief stop to drop off a refrigerator at the dock of a single house or picking up a letter delivered by speedboat, a vacationer gets off on an isolated island in the Broken Group with a canoe rented from the steamship company, it's all part of the boat's daily run to serve any spot that can be reached in Barkley Sound and the vessel is an integral part of west coast living.

The Broken Group of islands, etched with paperwhite beaches and clear turquoise waters, chokes the reaches of Barkley Sound like a spray of diamonds and provides for those lucky enough to launch their boats out of Toquart Bay, at the head of the sound, or to travel on the Lady Rose, a magical destination of pristine solitude to be shared only with the rasping cries of the mystical black raven and the frolicsome company of seals and sea lions.

The once numerous Indian summer fishing camps are now deserted and the delight of this place remains to be gathered through the solitude, the camera and the taste of being there.

On the sound's western shore the Bamfield Inlet becomes the sheltered main street for the village of Bamfield. This is the end of a long unpaved road (if you are driving) and the start of the rugged and challenging 72km West Coast Trail for those more adventurous hikers. The trail starts from the lighthouse at Cape Beale and was originally the lifesaving trail for shipwrecked sailors on a coastline noted for its marine tragedy. For the less hardy, beautiful beaches and meandering trails provide excellent views and photographic opportunities. The Bamfield Marine Biological Station is a place of research and teaching located on the site of what was the trans-Pacific submarine telegraph cable station. From lessons learned practical projects are underway to farm the sea for seaweed and shellfish.

At the northwest corner of the inlet, at it's most exposed extreme, lies the fishing village of Ucluelet, hidden inside a long finger of safe water and reached by paved road from Port Alberni. On the coastal plain between Ucluelet and Tofino to the north, lies the Long Beach portion of Pacific Rim National Park, an expanse of beach, surf, rocklands and luxuriant rain forest, juxtaposing the images of peace and power. This is a place where nature exhibits its changes and immensities and leaves us standing in awe. The wide white sandy shores with their tidal rim of bleached stranded forest giants washed up by the towering winter gales, stretch endlessly here, only punctuated by sea-worn rocky towers and trees twisted and tortured by the winds. These are beaches beyond compare. The long intertidal zone around rocks and cliffs provides a blaze of colour and life in the clear cold pools. During the summer and at times of their yearly migration, grey whales are sighted off the shore, giving a sense of thrill and wonder that highlights an amazing environment.

On a narrow neck of land at the end of the road Tofino looks out over the waters of Clayoquot Sound, the great untouched stands of Pacific coast forest on Meares Island and a whole new world of tiny jagged islands as far as the eye can see.

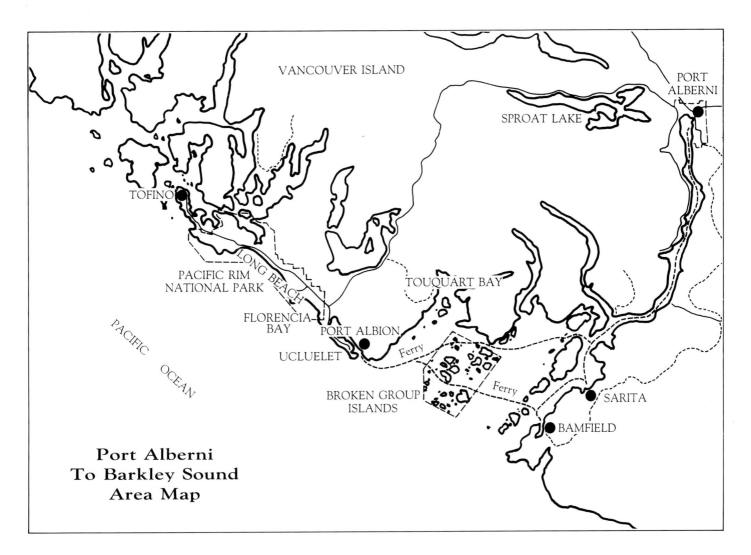

**Port Alberni
To Barkley Sound
Area Map**

## Bamfield

### What To See And Do:

Boating, fishing, and driving. Bamfield is the gateway to the Westcoast Trail, the northern trail head being 5km east at Pachena Bay. Part of the Pacific Rim National Park, the Trail is a 6-8 day wilderness hike for the hardy and experienced. It travels for 72km along rugged coastline to its southern head at Port Renfrew. or further information contact the information centre on Highway 4 (summer), or the Park Office near Wikannish: or write The Superintendent, Pacific Rim National Park, Box 280, Ucluelet, B.C. V0R 3A0. Visitor Information: Bamfield Chamber of Commerce, P.O. Box 5, Bamfield, B.C. V0R 1B0.

### How To Get there:

**By Car:** 90km gravel road from Port Alberni, of 105km gravel road from Cowichan/Youbou. **By Ferry:** M.V. Lady Rose from Port Alberni three times weekly (passengers only.) **By Air:** Pacific Rim Airlines from Port Alberni or Vancouver ☎ Vancouver 224-4398, Port Alberni 724-4495.

### How To Get Around:

**Water Taxi,Boat Charters,Boat and Canoe Rentals:** Kingfisher Charters ☎ 728-3228; C.D. Charles Marine Charter Service 728-3282. **Boat Launching:** Port Desire.

### Where To Stay And Eat:

Aguilar House Resort ☎ 728-3323; Bamfield Trails Motel ☎ 728-3231. Wheelhouse Cafe.

# Port Alberni

*right:*

*The majestic shores of the Bamfield area are livened by rich tidepools and their often minute inhabitants.*

## How to get there:

**By car:** From Victoria north on Highway 1 to Nanaimo (112km,) or from Vancouver via B.C. Ferries (Horseshoe Bay) to Nanaimo; then north from Nanaimo on Highway 19 to Parksville, and west on Highway 4 (82km). Or from Prince Rupert via B.C. Ferries to Port Hardy, then south on Highway 19 to Parksville, and west on Highway 4 (384km from Port Hardy.) **By Bus:** Pacific Coach Lines from Vancouver, Victoria or Nanaimo ☎ Victoria 385-4411, or Vancouver 683-9277. **By Air:** Pacific Rim Airlines from Vancouver ☎ Vancouver 224-4398.

## How To Get Around:

**City Bus Transit** ☎ 723-3341. Orient Stage Lines: Port Alberni to Ucluelet and Tofino ☎ Alberni 723-6924. Alberni Marine Transportation Co. (M.V. Lady Rose) coastal vessel from Port Alberni to Bamfield, and to Ucluelet through Broken Group Islands ☎ Alberni 723-8313. **Taxis:** Alberni District United Cabs ☎ 723-2121; Fairway Taxi ☎ 723-3511 **Car Rentals:** Budget Rent-A-Car & Truck ☎ 724-4511. **Boat Charter/Rental:** Clutesi Haven Marina ☎ 723-8022; China Creek Marina ☎ 723-9812; Hunter's Marina ☎ 724-4244; and others. **Boat Launching:** Clutesi Haven Marina, Sproat Lake Prov. PArk, Ark Resort, China Creek Park. **Diving Rentals:** Alberni Divers ☎ 724-5255. **Horses:** Deer Creek Ranch ☎ 723-5802. **Air Charters/Tours:** Pacific Rim Airlines ☎ 724-4495.

## Where To Stay And Eat:

Timber Lodge Motor Inn with pool, dining ☎ 723-9415; Tyee Village Motel with pool, dining ☎ 723-8133; and others. Redford Motor Inn Recreational Vehicle Park ☎ 724-0121. Camping at Stamp Falls and Sproat Lake Provincial Parks. Campground & trailer park at China Creek Marina ☎ 723-9812; and others. Courtyard Restaurant in Timber Lodge Motor Inn for steak, seafood and prime rib ☎ 723-9415; Canal Restaurant for Greek food with a canal view ☎ 724-6555.

## What To Do And See:

Visit the Alberni Harbour Quay for the farmers' market, fresh seafood, handicrafts, and a viewing tower. Tour Alberni's deep sea port through the Harbour Commission ☎ 723-5312, or take a day long cruise on the M.V. Lady Rose as she serves the coastal communities on Barcley Sound, or drop off canoeists at the Broken Group Islands ☎ 723-8313. Visit the Alberni Valley Museum for hands-on displays of local history and travelling exhibits; the Rollin Art Centre for displays of local arts and crafts and a small craft store; or the Robertson Creek Salmon Hatchery for a guided tour or to enjoy the walking trails. The J.V. Clyne Bird Sanctuary allows easy access for bird watchers. Mill tours may be taken of the Alberni Pulp and Paper Division ☎ 723-2161 (Wednesdays), or of the Alberni Pacific Sawmill ☎ 724-6511 (Thursdays). Take a Spring or Fall tour of the Mars Water Bombers at Sproat Lake ☎ 723-6225. Sproat Lake Provincial Park is for swimming and boating, or visiting the Indian petroglyphs along part of the shoreline; Stamp Falls Provincial Park features a waterfall, trails and fish ladders. Mt. Arrowsmith Regional Park features excellent hiking and skiing. Alberni is noted for its fishing — both saltwater and freshwater in local lakes and rivers. Nine-hole golf at Alberni Golf Club ☎ 723-5422, or Pleasant Valley Golf Course ☎ 724-5333. Tennis courts are located at several of the secondary schools and at Sproat Lake and Cherry Creek Recreational Centres. Echo Swimming Pool is on Wallace Street ☎ 723-8121. Racquet Ball Club ☎ 723-5922. Local Festivals include Loggers' Sports Day. Highland Dance Meet – June; Folkfest, Sproat Lake Water Festival of Sports – July; Salmon Festival and Derby – Labour Day Weekend.

**Visitor Information:** Box 190, Port Alberni, V9Y 7M7. ☎ 724-6535.

## Ucluelet, Long Beach, Tofino

### How To Get There:

**By Car:** Highway 4 west from Port Alberni (98km to Ucluelet/125km to Tofino.) **By Bus:** Orient Stage Lines from Port Alberni ☎ 723-6924. **By Air:** Pacific Rim Airlines from Vancouver or Port Alberni ☎ Vancouver 224-4398, Port Alberni 724-4495. By Ferry: Alberni Marine Transportation Co. (M.V. Lady Rose) Passengers only from Port Alberni to Ucluelet ☎ Port Alberni 723-8313.

### How To Get Around:

**Taxis:** Coastal Cabs ☎ 726-4262; Ucluelet Taxi ☎ 726-4213. **Car Rentals:** Avis – Ozzard Services ☎ 726-4451; Budget – Noel Enterprises ☎ 726-4221. **Boat Charters/Rentals:** Canadian Princess ☎ Ucluelet 726-7771; Subtidal Adventures ☎ Ucluelet 726-7061; Bayshore Marina – ☎ Ucluelet 726-7735; Sea Fun Charters ☎ Tofino 725-4229; Noah's Ark Boat Rentals ☎ Tofino 725-4225 (also canoes). Sightseeing and scuba cruises are offered by Subtidal Adventures. **Boat Launching:** Ucluelet – Foot of Bay Street, Government dock, and Seaplane Base Road. Tofino – Fisherman's Float. **Air Charters:** Pacific Rim Airlines ☎ Tofino 725-3295; Long Beach Helicopters ☎ Tofino 725-3312.

### Where To Stay And Eat:

Heavy tourist demand and limited accommodation make it advisable to phone ahead from Port Alberni. Canadian Princess Floating Hotel/Resort is a converted steamship moored in Ucluelet Harbour. Dining, lounge. Daily fishing, diving, nature cruises. Also package tours from Vancouver and Seattle ☎ Ucluelet 726-7771. West Coast Motel, pool, harbour view ☎ Ucluelet 726-7732; MacKenzie Beach Resort ☎ Tofino 725-3439; Pacific Sands Beach Resort ☎ Tofino 725-3322; Clayoquot Lodge, Private Island Resort on Stubbs Island ☎ 725-3284; B & B:Burleys ☎ Ucluelet 726-4444. Camping at Ucluelet Campgrounds ☎ 726-7511; MacKenzie Beach Resort; Pacific Rim National Park Green Point Campground & Schooner Campground (primitive). The Whale's Tale Restaurant Thornton Motel ☎ 726-4621; Canadian Princess, view dining ☎ 726-7771 (both in Ucluelet). The Loft, seafood ☎ Tofino 725-4241.

### What To See And To Do:

Visit the salmon hatchery at Port Albion, or the Canadian Coast Guard Centre at Amphritite Point. Shop for native arts at Duquah Gallery ☎ 726-7223 or local artists' work at Sandiper Art Centre ☎ 726-7331. Visit Pacific Rim National Park (Long Beach Unit and Broken Group Islands.) The Long Beach Unit consists of over 20km of sandy beaches and rocky points open to the Pacific Ocean. Picnic sites are located at Florencia Bay, Wikaninnish Beach, Combers Beach, Long Beach, and Radar Hill View Point. Hike the beaches and headlands, boat or surf fish, scuba dive one of the best areas in the world, or join in the park interpretation programs. In the Spring take one of the whale watching cruises from Ucluelet. Explore the Broken Group Islands by canoe or kyak (Access via M.V. Lady Rose from Port Alberni).

Use marine charts for the Islands. **Full information** from the Superintendent, Pacific Rim National Park, Box 280, Ucluelet, B.C., V0R 3A0, or from the Park Office near Wikannish.

**Visitor Information:** Ucluelet Chamber of Commerce, P.O. Box 428, Ucluelet, B.C., V0R 3A0

Northern Vancouver Island

*Friendly Cove:*
Kayaks now skim the waters where Captain Cook
first landed on the northwest shores, on a voyage
of discovery.

*Bella Bella:*
Isolated from the mainland highway system the small communities around Bella Bella celebrate the weekly visits of the ferry service.

*Northern Sound:*
The early morning light has a specialness here.

*Northern Sound:*
The thick clouds lay like white ropes binding the still sleeping land.

*Bute Inlet:*
Water-falls tumble from the very sky in this spot
favoured by fishermen.

*Fitz Hugh Sound, Lighthouse:*
A tiny oasis of man's technology and daring,
almost ignored by the passing passengers.

*Cortes Marina, Cortes Island:*
A secluded cove, a place to fish and relax with
only the cry of the gulls to break the silence.

*Sointula:*
The rain squalls of the night abated, and in the
cool morning light the harbour shone like
burnished pewter

*Community of Church House:*
Small fishing villages tucked into isolated bays
breed a special type of person and a warmth for
passing strangers.

*Herriot Bay, Fisherman:*
For many who venture this way the gold of the
ocean is an addictive lure. Patience and a long
fight won this one, where many were lost before.

*The Queen of the North:*
Blustering through the narrow passages, a time to
travel, a time to relax, with the view slipping
quietly past.

*The Inside Passage:*
Our sister ship passes us going south and we rush
to the rails in the evening light, to wave, or just
to feel the sun's last rays.

# The Comox Valley

Here is a valley steeped in history. Coal was discovered here over one hundred years ago. Coal, a most highly sort after commodity, to fuel the British Navy's fleet in the Pacific; and almost overnight Cumberland, with its get-rich-quick entrepreneurs and transient miners, along with a large population of imported Chinese labour, became a thriving city of ten thousand people. Coal became King in this valley of beautiful woods and lakes.

Today the nature of the Valley's way of life is much changed and the dependance on coal is gone. Fishing, forestry, and farming, providing sustenance to the economy, are now joined by tourism as the range of local natural resources is discovered by coastal travellers.

From the crystal clear tide-waters, abounding in invertebrate life that will woo divers from around the world; Forbidden Plateau, covered with flowers through the summer months and a skiers' paradise in the winter; the valley is a year around magnet for naturalists and those who just like to be outdoors. Trails for the novice and expert abound through the area and are generally well marked and easy of grade. Wonderful lakes can be reached on short day hikes and the views over the mountains and the Strait of Georgia can be breathtaking. Fishing in both fresh and salt water is outstanding.

There are three major communities in the Valley, the largest of which is Courtnay, a cosmopolitan centre with excellent accommodations and restaurants. Courtnay, its streets decked with flowers, has become world renowned for the scope and quality of its Summer Arts Festival, with a wide range of performing, visual and literary arts planned from March to September. There is always a treat in store for visitors with music from opera to jazz, plays, a Renaissance Fair, and exhibitions and demonstrations of many many crafts and skills. The Youth Music Centre has Canada-wide attracted students to perform under the finest leadership and provides a musical core to the festival.

Comox, where it all started, still boasts one of the earliest buildings erected in the area: the *Lorne Hotel* which was built in 1867. Today the town plays host to a major Canadian Air Force base, while the neat and well protected harbour, behind Goose Spit, with the historic H.M.C.S. Quadra naval base is an interesting port serving the fleet of trollers and shellfish boats that ply these plankton rich local waters.

Cumberland, which just a few years ago was a neglected ghost town, has now a new lease on life and is growing with the overall population expansion of the area. fortunately, pride in the early history of the area has ensured that the unique buildings remain with the new and a district museum building draws people passing bye to resavor the interesting heritage.

## How To Get Around.

**Taxi:** United Cabs serves Comox Valley area ☎ 338-7727. **Bus:** Hilo Transportation to Mt. Washington and Forbidden Plateau ski areas ☎ 334-2544. **Car rental:** Budget Rent-a-Car ☎ 338-7717; Rent-a-Wreck ☎ 334-2060; R.V. Rentals ☎ 334-4428. **Boat charters/rentals:** Nighthawk Charters ☎ 339-4692; Gordon Greer Ltd, sail and power cruises ☎ 339-4914; Bates Beach Resort ☎ 334-2151; Canoes, kayaks, surfers from Freewind Rentals. Boat Launch: Courtenay Marina, Comox Marina, Point Homes, Kin Beach, King Coho and Bates Beach Marinas, and Comox Airport. **Bicycles:** Rent-all Equipment ☎ 334-3678. **Scuba diving:** T.D. Sports, rentals and charters ☎ 338-1633. **Ski equipment:** Ski Tak Hut ☎ 334-2537; Vancouver Is. Ski Services ☎ 338-9033. **Horses:** Jumping Jodpurs ☎ 335-0069; Norwood Equestrian Centre ☎ 334-3678. **Air charter:** Coval Air Charters ☎ 339-6711.

**Visitor Information:** Courtenay — Comox Chamber of Commerce, 2040 Cliff Ave., Courtenay ☎ 334-3234.

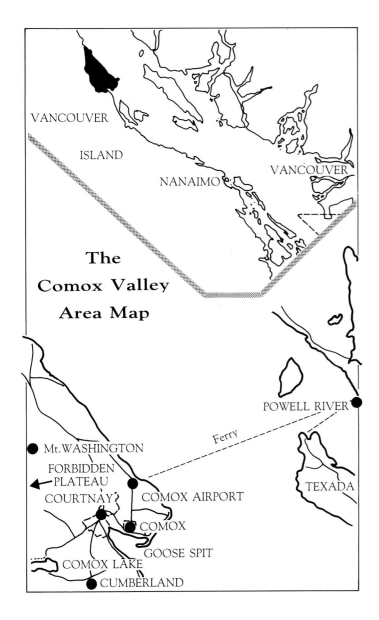

**The Comox Valley Area Map**

## How To Get There.

**By car:** Ministry of Highways ferry Powell River to Comox (1¼hrs), then 6.5km west to Courtenay. Or Highway 19 108km north from Nanaimo. Or Highway 19 281km south from Port Hardy. **By bus:** Pacific Coach Lines from Vancouver via Nanaimo, or from Vancouver Island points ☎ Vancouver 280-9439 or Victoria 385-4411. **By Rail:** VIA Rail to Courtenay from Victoria and way points ☎ Victoria 385-4411. **By Air:** Pacific Western Airlines to Comox ☎ Vancouver 684-6161; Air B.C. ☎ Victoria 388-5151.

## Where To Stay And Eat.

**Courtenay:** The Westerly Hotel ☎ 338-7741; the Washington Inn ☎ 338-5441; and others. **Comox:** Port Augusta Motel ☎ 339-2277; and others. King Coho Resort and Marina campground and trailer park ☎ 339-4154. Miracle Beach Provincial Park approx. 25km north on Highway 19. Gourmet Dining: The Old House Restaurant; William Van Horne. French: La Cremaillere. European and seafood: Gaff Rig. Arbutus Hotel, Seaside Restaurant and others.

## What To Do And See.

Canadian Forces Base at Comox. Swimming and picnicking at Kye Bay and Goose Spit. Also excellent windsurfing at Goose Spit (or Comox Lake). Filberg Lodge is a heritage building exhibiting works of artists and crafts people, while Filberg Lodge features a hands-on animal farm for children. Courtenay Museum is a log building housing exhibits of early settlers and native Indian culture, logging and mining displays, and an international doll collection. Cumberland Museum contains a model of a coal mine, and displays the former Chinatown. Century Box Museum features 100 years of police and military history. The Forbidden Plateau and Mt. Washington, within 35min. of Courtenay, are top notch downhill and cross country ski areas, and in summer offer excellent hiking. Also hiking to Moat and Circlet Lakes, Alone Mountain and Mt. Becher. At Puntledge River Fish Hatchery salmon fry (early summer) and adult fish (fall) are on display. There is good saltwater fishing, or trout fishing in Comox Lake; the Comox Valley Fishing Guides Association can be contacted through the Courtenay Chamber of Commerce. Take a 1 to 3 day cruise aboard a commercial troller ☎ 338-1986. Comox Recreation Centre offers 1-week sailing courses aimed at vacationers. The celebrated Courtenay Youth Summer Music Centre is an International School presenting musical productions from jazz to symphony, opera and dance throughout the summer months. **For golf:** Sunnydale Golf Club ☎ 334-3342; Comox Golf Club ☎ 339-7272. **For tennis:** 7 courts in Comox and 6 in Courtenay. **Local Festivals:** Winter Carnival – Feb; Renaissance Fair – July; Fall Fair – Sept.

# Discovery Passage To Nootka Sound

## Campbell River

Campbell River is located at approximately the midpoint of the east coast of Vancouver Island where two systems of tidal flows meet, flowing in and out of Johnstone Strait to the north, and Georgia Strait to the south. It is perhaps these complex water actions and the narrow passages between islands that make Campbell River a challenging and world famous fishing hot spot. Between a scatter of islands and a splatter of lakes, Campbell River has a wealth of recreational temptations. Seymour Narrows where once a notorious navigational hazard, the submerged Ripple Rock, was removed with a tremendous dynamite blast in 1958, is now a focus for the ardent fisherman as well as a major scuba diving attraction. Not far away Mittlenatch Island bird sanctuary is a naturalist's treat although reached by boat only. Close at hand starts the Elk Falls Provincial Park, and the alpine wilderness of Strathcona Provincial Park in the centre of Vancouver Island, where steep ridges and snow fields lead the eyes up from the countless rivers, lakes and forest slopes.

Campbell River itself provides the full range of visitor facilities. It is a good check point for trips north or west, a good place to stock up on supplies and a good centre for hiking, kayaking or just enjoying the diversity of nature. Quadra is the best known of the Discovery Islands. Although only a brief 15 minute ferry ride from Campbell River, it is nevertheless an island of seclusion and character. During the gold rush in the 1860's, it was proposed that a rail-line could be built from Quadra Island and up Bute Inlet to provide a shorter route to the Cariboo gold fields than the Fraser Canyon. At the time of that vision, settlers around Campbell River actually went over to Quadra to obtain their supplies.

Cape Mudge Lighthouse is at the south tip of Quadra and the boulder-strewn beach near the lighthouse is one of the island sites where Indian petroglyphs have been found, with designs of marine animals pounded into intertidal rocks, leaving us today to only wonder and speculate on the history and purpose of these rock pictures. The Kwakiutl Museum shows roughly half of the traditional potlatch material that was confiscated in 1922 when the potlatch ceremonies were banned and which was returned to the coastal peoples only in 1979 at Cape Mudge and 1980 in Alert Bay. Another favoured place on Quadra is the lonely and beautiful Rebecca Spit on the east side of the island.

Cortes is an island of peacefulness. It takes just a 45 minute ferry crossing from Heriot Bay on Quadra Island to reach Whaletown on Cortes which was the first whaling base of the B.C. Whaling Co. The east side of the island across from Desolation Sound at the top of the Sunshine Coast is a favourite place of yachtsmen and the island has several marine resorts and five red government wharves for visiting boats. Hague Lake has white sandy beaches with fresh water swimming, for a change, and visitors enjoy the two seashore parks at Manson's Landing and Smelt Bay.

To the west, Gold River is a logging and milling establishment, 88 km from Campbell River and deep in the inlets slashed within Vancouver Island. The paved road threads by the lakes and mountains of Strathcona Park, the first B.C. provincial park, where the Park Lodge offers tranquil lakeside accommodations and can provide a wide range of trips, courses or other outdoor activities.

Friendly Cove at the blustering Pacific entrance of Nootka Sound, is an important historic site because it was there where Captain Cook made the first white man contact with the native west coast people when, in 1778 he arrived with the ships Resolution and Discovery. At that time about 1500 people lived at the summer village called Yuquot and it is hard to imagine today the bustle of people in cedar long houses and canoes that he must have found. Now, the

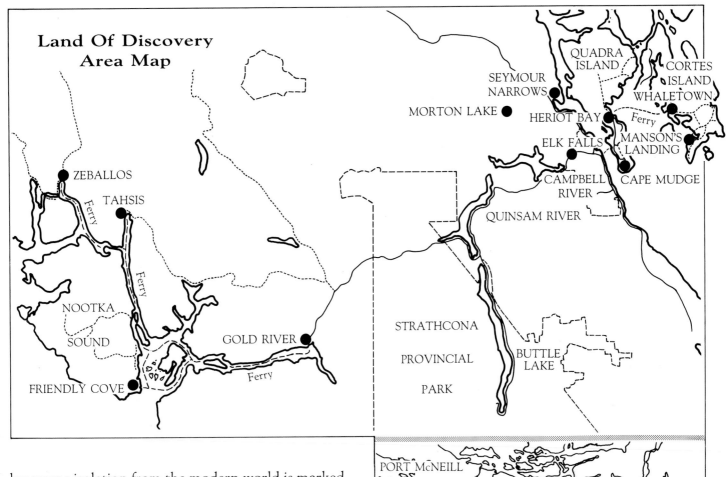

**Land Of Discovery Area Map**

SEYMOUR NARROWS
QUADRA ISLAND
CORTES ISLAND
WHALETOWN
MORTON LAKE
HERIOT BAY
Ferry
ZEBALLOS
TAHSIS
Ferry
Ferry
ELK FALLS
MANSON'S LANDING
CAMPBELL RIVER
CAPE MUDGE
QUINSAM RIVER
NOOTKA
SOUND
GOLD RIVER
Ferry
STRATHCONA
PROVINCIAL
PARK
BUTTLE LAKE
FRIENDLY COVE

PORT McNEILL
VANCOUVER ISLAND
CAMPBELL RIVER

lonesome isolation from the modern world is marked by a single totem pole and the pale steeple of a Catholic church donated by the Spanish government. A long pebble beach on the ocean side of the village opens up to the horizon of the Pacific Ocean. Only the timeless beauty of nature remains, a witness of human dramas.

For an adventure on the west coast, the MV Uchuck makes afternoon cruises to Friendly Cove in the summer. Travelling down Muchalat Arm from Gold River, the ship emerges from the fjord scenery of plunging cliffs, to the islands and scattered empty beaches at the mouth of the sound, and throughout the year she makes overnight trips to Tahsis, stopping at various logging camps as needs demand. Through skinny Tahsis Narrows, the Uchuck services the settlements in Esperanza Inlet and up the long slit of water to Zeballos an antique of a gold-mining town that still retains a colouful frontier appearance with the old style Zeballos Hotel.

**Visitor information:** Chamber of Commerce Convention Bureau, P.O. Box 400, Campbell River, V9W 5B6 ☎ 286-0764.

Gold River Tourist Co-operative, Box 610, Gold River, B.C., V0P 1G0 ☎ 283-7421. Information for Zeballos from the Village Office, Box 127, Zeballos, B.C., V0P 2A0 ☎ 761-4229 (Tues-Fri a.m.).

# Campbell River

## How To Get There.

**By Car:** Highway 19 156km. north from Nanaimo (266km. north from Victoria), or 237km. south from Port Hardy. **By Bus:** Pacific Coach Lines from Vancouver ☎ 683-9277 and from Victoria ☎ 385-4411, and from Port Hardy. **By Air:** Pacific Western Airlines ☎ 684-6161 (Vanc.), or 388-5191 (Victoria); Air B.C. ☎ 685-3211 (Vanc.)

*View from the wheelhouse of one of the B.C. Ferries threading through the narrow waters.*

## How To Get Around.

**Ferry:** Ministry of Highways ferry to Quadra and Cortes Islands. **Bus:** Campbell River Transit System ☎ 287-7433 Cortes connection ☎ 935-6324 on Cortes Island. **Taxi:** Atwater Cabs ☎ 286-6236; Bee-Line Taxi ☎ 287-8383. Bus charter and limousine service to the airport: Wayfinder Limousine and Bus Charters ☎ 286-1200. **Car rental:** Budget ☎ 923-4283; Rent-a-Wreck ☎ 287-8353. **Boat rentals:** The Dolphin Resort ☎ 287-3066; Painter's Lodge Resort ☎ 286-1102 (also charters). **Boat charters:** North Island Charters ☎ 287-3137; Sea Ray Charters ☎ 287-9820; and others. **Boat Launch:** Oyster Bay, Willow Point, Ken Forde Gas Station, The Spit and others. **Diving rentals:** Seafun Divers Ltd. ☎ 287-3622. **Wind surfing rentals:** Wind Surfing School, Willow Point ☎ 923-3113. **Bicycle Rentals:** Silly Willy's Bicycles, Willow Point ☎ 923- 7161. **Air Charter:** Air Nootka ☎ 800-232-6326 toll free, also scheduled flights to Gold River and Tahsis; CoVal Air Ltd ☎ 287-8371, also scheduled flights to Vancouver Harbour and local and north coast communities; Okanagan Helicopters ☎ 286-6118.

## Where To Stay And Eat.

The Famous Painter's Lodge and Fishing Resort, also marine view dining ☎ 286-1102; The Island Inn ☎ 923-4241; and others. Silver King Trailer Park ☎ 286-6142; Elk Falls and Morton Lake Provincial Campgrounds. For elegant dining, Le Chateau Briand ☎ 287- 4143; Shagpoke's Restaurant at the Anchor Inn ☎ 287-8923; Austrian Chalet ☎ 923-4231.

## What To Do And See.

Visit the Quinsam River Salmon Hatchery, picnic area and nature trails; also the canyon, falls and dam at Elk Falls Park. Ripple Rock Lookout boasts a panoramic view of the boats battling the currents of Seymour Narrows especially on the changing tide. Campbell River Museum displays Indian artifacts and historic exhibits. Elk Falls Mill, and Western Mines (south of Buttle Lake) each offer tours, or see the John Hart Generating Station 4km west along the Gold River Highway. Further along this highway is Strathcona Provincial Park, 500,000 acres mostly in wilderness, offering fresh water fishing and swimming, boating and hiking. Just outside the park itself is Strathcona Park Lodge which is both a resort and a school offering adventure holidays, wilderness leadership, and youth packages ☎ operator (area 604) and ask for Strathcona Lodge, identity #N693546. Twenty kilometres east of Campbell River is Mitlenatch Island Bird Sanctuary, nesting grounds for thousands of seabirds, and accessible by private boat or charter. Take an aerial sightseeing tour or enjoy excellent scuba diving. Strathcona Gardens recreation centre features arena, pool and *The Salmon Capital Of The World*. Local Festivals: Salmon Festival — July; Salmon Derby — August.

# Quadra and Cortes Islands

## How To Get There.

**By Car:** Ministry of Highways ferry from Campbell River to Quathiaski Cove on Quadra Island (15min.); and from Heriot Bay (Quadra Island) to Whaletown on Cortes Island (40min.) **By Bus:** Cortes Connection ☎ 935-6324 (Cortes). **By Air:** CoVal Air ☎ 287-8371 (Campbell River.)

## How To Get Around.

**Taxi:** Tony's Taxi, Quadra Island ☎ 285-3598. **Boat rentals/charters:** Quadra Island — April Point Lodge; Quadra Resort ☎ 285-3450; Heriot Bay Inn ☎ 285-3322. Fishing guides available through all four resorts. On Cortes Island Contact Glen Carison for fishing and diving charters, and cruises in Desolation Sound ☎ 935-6421.

## Where To Stay And Eat.

**Quadra Island:** April Point Lodge, with marine view dining, complete fishing packages ☎ 285-3329; and the other above-mentioned resorts. The Heriot Bay Inn has a restaurant and pub. The Neighbourhood Pub, home cooked meals ☎ 285-3713; also The Coffee Stop. **Cortes Island:** The Cortes Bay Marine Resort has housekeeping cottages and a snack bar ☎ 935-6361. There is camping at Rebecca Spit Provincial Marine Park on Quadra; and also close to Manson's Landing Park on Cortes.

## What To Do And See.

There is good beachcombing and clam digging, as well as excellent salmon fishing. Most popular beach on Quadra is Rebecca Spit, and on Cortes, Manson's Landing Park. The Kwakiutl Native Museum at the Indian village of Cape Mudge (southern tip of Quadra Island) has a fine display of potlatch regalia, and across from the museum local petroglyphs are displayed. Other petroglyphs may be found at their original site on the beach by the Cape Mudge Lighthouse.

**Visitor Information:** Contact the Chamber of Commerce, Campbell River.

# Gold River, Tahsis, Zeballos.

## How To Get There.

**By Car:** Gold River — 88km west of Campbell River on Highway 28; Tahsis — a further 50 km northwest of Gold River along a secondary road; Zeballos — 130km north of Campbell River along Highway 19, and then a further 60km north and west along restricted roads. **By Bus:** Ross Gold River Taxi Cabs from Campbell River to Gold River ☎ 283-7314 (Campbell River). Port McNeill Stage and Limousine Service from Port McNeill to Zeballos ☎ 956-4432 (Port McNeill). **By Air:** Air Nootka, charter and scheduled service to Gold River and Tahsis ☎ 800-232-6326 (Campbell River toll free); Pacific Rim Airlines, charter and scheduled services from Vancouver and Port Alberni to Tahsis — ☎ 224-4398 (Vancouver), or 734-4495 (Port Alberni). Air B.C. to Zeballos ☎ 388-5151 (Victoria) or 685-3211 (Vancouver).

## How To Get Around.

**By Ferry:** Nootka Sound Service Ltd. (M.V. Uchuck) serving Gold River, Tahsis, Nootka, Zeballos and Port Eliza ☎ 283-2515 (Gold River). Tahsis Taxi to Gold River ☎ 934-7911 (Tahsis). **Boat Rental:** Nootka Sound Marina, Tahsis ☎ 934-6462. Boat launch: Gold River — Government Dock, Lions Wharf; Tahsis — Government Dock; Zeballos — Marina.

## Where To Stay And Eat.

Limited accommodation. Gold River Chalet, complete hotel facilities, heated pool, fishing guides, dining ☎ 283-2244. Peppercorn Trails Motel and R.V. Park, Gold River ☎ 283-2443. Tahsis Motel, licenced dining ☎ 934-6318; Tahsis Chalet, Licenced dining ☎ 934-6301. The Guest House, Zeballos ☎ 761-4351; The Zeballos Hotel, sleeping rooms ☎ 761-4275

## What To See And Do.

Take a cruise on the M.V. Uchuck which includes a visit to Friendly Cove (first discovered by Captain Cook). Strathcona Provincial Wilderness Park and the outstanding Strathcona Park Lodge are nearby (see Campbell River). Try your luck panning for gold at Zeballos.

# Port McNeill

Port McNeil lies nestled in a quiet crook of land where the Nimpkish river flows out into Broughton Strait, sheltered by Malcolm Island to the north and by the tiny jewel of Cormorant Island to the east.

The full curve of McNeil Bay to the west of the town makes a fine afternoon's walk along the beach, with abounding crabs and clams for the evening supper pot or a tasty beach bake-out, leading around to the moonscape rocks at Ledge Point just across from the town.

Deep in the protection of Beaver Cove, named for the famous Hudson Bay 110 foot paddle-wheeler, the first steam vessel on the B.C. coast, is the tiny board-walk community of Telegraph Cove, built out over the water on piles, with its photogenic old houses reflecting in the waters alongside the bright colours of the fishing fleet.

Tucked into the arc of Cormorant Island, Alert Bay is a fishing village with quaintness, character and a significant centre for both the revitalization and preservation of the native culture. Kwakiutl people from the Nimpkish River formed the community in 1870 when a salmon saltery was established at Alert Bay and the U'mista Cultural Centre exhibits part of the historic Potlatch Collection where under the massive wood beams, the open display of worn and used ceremonial gear make the surrealistic seem close and real. Totem poles look west over the water and the town boasts one totem pole that is the tallest in the world at 173 ft high. Within walking distance, the ecological park Gator Gardens has a boardwalk through the peculiar landscape of bog and swamps.

Sointula means "a place of harmony" and a utopian society was the aim of the original settlers from Finland. Land on Malcolm Island was granted for the establishment of a cooperative community. Even though an organized utopia has not flourished, the people of Sointula still show the blond hair and blue eye traits of Finns and houses and gardens seem to have a special air of tidiness, care and thought. The Sointula Co-op Store has been the supplier of daily and maritime needs since 1909. While Malcolm Island is much bigger than the adjacent Cormorant Island, the Indians did not live on this island because, as the legend says, it emerged out of the sea and inevitably would go back under.

## What To Do And See.

### Port McNeill:

Walk to the head of McNeill Bay to view the sea life, or hunt for crabs or clams. Talk to Helen Scott at Craft Corner about how to find local historic sites. Enjoy oceanside or wilderness camping. If travelling on restricted roads be sure to obtain road maps and obey signs, i.e. the Keogh Mainline logging road form Port McNeill to Port Alice passes dozens of lakes. Take a ferry ride to Alert Bay and Sointula. Try wreck diving at Crocker Rock or Bates Passage. Take a whale watching cruise on the M.V. Gikuma to Robson Bight ecological reserve through Stubbs Island Charters ☎ 928-3185. See the world's largest burl(22.5 tons) 2 miles west of Port McNeill. There is an outdoor pool and arena complex in town. For golf see Port Hardy. Local Festivals: May Days; Novice Loggers' Sports -July.

### Alert Bay:

Visit the Kwakiutl longhouse, the Alert Bay Library/Museum featuring native artifacts and displays on early settlement. The Indian cemetery and totem poles are of interest, as is the 173 foot totem claimed to be the tallest in the world. Two historic buildings are the 100-year old Anglican Church and the St George's Hospital Chapel. U'mista Cultural Centre contains a comprehensive collection of Kwakiutl artifacts. Gator Gardens Ecological Park has nature trails and a board walk. Shop for native art and crafts at Art Class Gallery. Local festivals: May Day, Indian June Sports.

### Sointula:

Visit the Petroglyphs at Mitchell Bay. The Finnish Cultural Museum displays artifacts of early settlers.

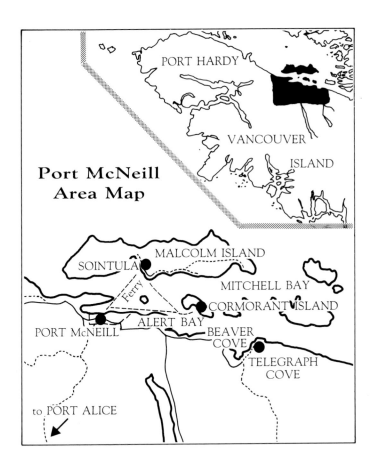

**Port McNeill Area Map**

## How To Get Around.

### Port McNeill:

Port Alice Limousine Services from Port Hardy Airport to Port Alice with connections to Port McNeill ☎ 284-3568. Ministry of Highways ferry, or Gulf Air Ltd., to Sointula and Alert Bay. Port McNeill Taxi, and also service to Zeballos on the west coast by Port McNeill Stage and Limousine Service — For both services ☎ 956-4432. **Boat charters/rentals:** Independent Charter Boat Referals Ltd. for fishing, sailing, and sightseeing ☎ 956-3739; Northwind Charters ☎ 956-3410. **Diving charters:** DeLisle's Diving Den ☎ 956-3410. Boat launching: Gov't Wharf Breakwater. **Air charters:** Air B.C. at Port Hardy Airport ☎ 949-6353

### Alert Bay:

Bay Cabs ☎ 974-5510. Fishing Charters from Oceanview Camping and Trailer Park ☎ 974-5213. Boat launch: Fir Street near Government Wharf. Air charter: Minstrel Air, Alert Bay ☎ 974-5811

## How To Get There.

### Port McNeill:

**By Car:** Highway 19 389km north of Nanaimo, or 41km south of Port Hardy. **By bus:** Pacific Coach Lines from Vancouver and Vancouver Island points. **By Air:** Pacific Western Airlines and Air B.C., both at the Port Hardy Airport.

### Alert Bay (Cormorant Island).

**By car or on foot:** Ministry of Highways ferry from Port McNeill (Vancouver Island) — 90 min. **By Air:** Gulf Air from Port McNeill to Alert Bay.

### Sointula (Malcolm Island):

**By Car:** Ministry of Highways ferry from Port McNeill (Vancouver Island) — 90 min. **By Air.** Gulf Air from Port McNeill.

## Where To Stay And Eat.

### Port McNeill:

Haida-Way Inn, dining lounge, pub ☎ 956-3373; Dalewood Inn, dining and pub, fishing charters ☎ 956-3304. Bauza Cove Campground, best in the whole area with fishing guides, rentals, situated 27km south of Port McNeill at Telegraph Cove. The Cookhouse Restaurant on Broughton Blvd. is a local favorite ☎ 956-4933.

### Alert Bay:

Bayside Inn, bar ☎ 974-5770; Nimpkish Hotel, pub ☎ 974-5716. Oceanview Camping and Trailer Park.

### Sointula:

Beachcombers' Inn and Gourmandy Restaurant, group fishing charters and scuba diving arranged ☎ 973-6365. Hicks' Lodge, fishing lodge with cabins and dining facilities ☎ 973-6381. Sointula Co-op Store has a full range of groceries.

**Visitor information:** Port McNeill Chamber of Commerce, Box 728, Port McNeill, V0N 2R6.

Alert Bay Tourist Bureau, P.O. Box 28, Alert Bay. ☎ 974-5213

Port McNeill Chamber of Commerce, Box 728, Port McNeill, V0N 2R0

# Port Hardy and The Central Coast

At the northern-most point of the Vancouver Island Highway, Port Hardy is an important linking point between the north and central coasts of British Columbia and is a strategic centre for industry on the island's tip. Coal was the magnet that 150 years ago enticed the Hudson Bay Company to build Fort Rupert, and started the north island's development.

The ferries, Queen of the North and Queen of Prince Rupert, begin their summer journeys from here up the narrow reaches of the Inside Passage to Bella Bella, Prince Rupert and onward to the Queen Charlotte islands, while other boats and planes of all sizes fan out their services through the islands, bays and inlets in every direction.

Travelling west on land from Port Hardy, the west coast sea water is only 20 km away, at the former whaling village of Coal Harbour, where giant jawbones of a blue whale recall those long past activities. Today pods of killer whale exuberatly spout just off-shore in the Johnstone Strait.

A westward logging road from Port Hardy leads to the tiny and secluded village of Holberg, deep in the inlets that slash nearly through the island tip. One can sit on the porch of the Scarlet Ibis pub and look over the surging Pacific tides in Holberg Inlet although still a very many miles from the open Ocean. Going on through *Elephant Crossing* is the access for the trails to the 15,000 hectare wilderness of Cape Scott Provincial Park. This remote wind-swept area has remnants of an attempted settlement by early Danish pioneers, but the fierce elements of nature were too much for even those hardy settlers to succeed. The solitary sandy beach at San Josef Bay is well worth reaching through a short hike in the moss-covered rain forest. Those intent on exploring more of this park need to be prepared for very bad conditions and distances that may take several days to cover.

Bella Bella is the one central coast community where B.C. Ferries makes a scheduled stop. The houses of Bella Bella are aligned on the shores of Campbell Island which is entwined in a maze of channels and islands. Mills, mines and canneries are the major providers of income in this isolated region. Five kilometres away on Denny Island at the site of the World War II air base the new community of Shearwater hosts the scheduled airline service and provides a peaceful base for sport fishermen. Rivers Inlet, only accessible by charter boat or float plane, once produced the most prolific salmon runs' and five canneries operated in the area. These canneries have closed and now some have been converted into isolated but highly regarded fishing resorts. A number of fly-in resorts are found especially in Rivers and Knight Inlets. Tiny settlements exist in the twists and turns of the waterways, where time must be measured only by the patterns of nature.

Remote now from the centres of civilization, this area was actually the first reached from land by explorer Alexander MeKenzie in 1793. Nowadays, even the rock monument to MeKenzie at King Island takes a concerted effort to reach.

The gentle islands and inlets have been the traditional homes of the coastal native people. Old forgotten village sites crumble under nature's relentless advances. Totem poles and house posts lie skewed along the foreshore mantled in mosses, where few people will take the time and make the effort to travel. Beyond the shell-covered beaches, the land climbs more steeply and waterfalls drape the looming green slopes from mist-enveloped peaks.

**Tourist Information:** Port Hardy Chamber of Commerce, Box 249, Port Hardy, V0N 2P0 ☎ 949-7622.

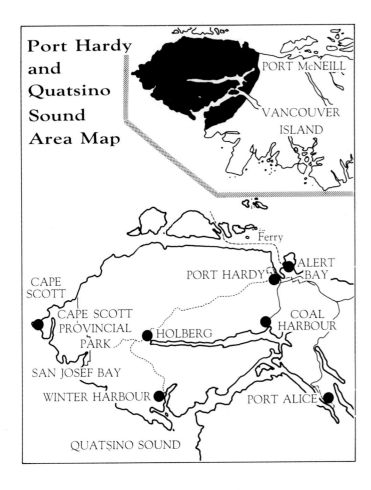

**Port Hardy and Quatsino Sound Area Map**

PORT McNEILL
VANCOUVER ISLAND
Ferry
PORT HARDY
ALERT BAY
CAPE SCOTT
CAPE SCOTT PROVINCIAL PARK
HOLBERG
COAL HARBOUR
SAN JOSEF BAY
WINTER HARBOUR
PORT ALICE
QUATSINO SOUND

## How To Get There.

**By Car:** Via Highway 19, 380km. north from Nanaimo. B.C. Ferries from Prince Rupert to Bear Cove (10km. from Pt. Hardy). B.C. Ferries from Tsawwassen (Vancouver) to Bear Cove (Summer only.) See Inside Passage. **By Bus:** Pacific Coach Lines from Vancouver and Vancouver Island points. **By Air:** Pacific Western Airlines from Vancouver (Van. ☎ 684-6161); Air B.C. from Victoria, Vancouver and north coast points (Vic. ☎ 388-5151).

## Where To Stay And Eat.

Port Hardy Inn, dining ☎ 949-8525; Thunderbird Inn, fishing/diving charters arranged ☎ 949-7767; The Pioneer Inn, and Snuggles Restaurant with open hearth cooking ☎ 949-7271. Sunny Sanctuary Campground, near tidal wildlife sanctuary ☎ 949-8111; Quatse River Campground ☎ 949-8233; and others.

## How To Get Around.

North Island Transportation Co. connects ferry terminal and airport to town. Also available for charter ☎ 949-6300. **Car Rental:** Budget Rent-a-Car ☎ 949-6442. **Taxi:** Island Cab ☎ 949-8294. H.S.W. Limo. Services- serves airport from Holberg ☎ 288-3454. **Water Taxis:** Top Island Diving Activities Ltd. provide scheduled service to logging camps, also sightseeing and fishing charters ☎ 949-8654; In Quatsino Sound, Frank Hole and Co., Coal Hbr. ☎ 949-6358. **Charter boats:** Pt. Hardy Charter Boat Association- charters and rentals for fishing and sightseeing ☎ 949-2628; Van Isle Charters ☎ 949-7431. **Boat launch:** Fisherman's Wharf, Storey's Beach, Bear Cove. **Diving charters:** North Island Diving and Water Sports ☎ 949-7133. **Wind surfing:** Chris Gregg ☎ 949-8322. **Air charters:** Air B.C. (Pt. Hardy 949-6353); Vancouver Island Helicopters offer sightseeing (Pt. Hardy 949-6605).

## What To Do And See.

Excellent lake, river and salt water fishing in the area. Also superb diving. Visit Cape Scott Provincial Park, 65km. from Port Hardy to hike either the San Josef Trail (45min. to San Josef Bay's spectacular beaches), or the rigorous Cape Scott Trail (wilderness hiking for the experienced only). Allow several days for the Cape Scott trek to explore Nels Bight and the Cape itself. Or canoe down the San Josef River to San Josef Bay (camping here). Take a 20min. drive to Coal Harbour on Quatsino Sound, site of an old whaling station. Port Hardy Museum has excellent rotating displays and exhibits of native artifacts. Stroll the waterfront park at the northern end of Market St. Study bird and wildlife at Holmgren Flats estuary. Quatse River offers a nature trail and fish hatchery and children's mini-farm. Beaver Harbour Park offers a fine beach, trail and fishing. Good wind surfing at Hardy Bay or Storey's Beach. The Recreation Centre features indoor swimming, fitness and ice arena ☎ 949-6686. Golf at Seven Hills on the Port Alice Highway- Radio Through the operator N687943.

**Local Festivals:** Filomi Days, Aug., celebrates fishing, logging and mining in the area.

# The Northern Waters

*Mosquito Lake: Birches and Bog*
In a narrow cut valley the dappled silver skins of
the trees gleamed softly above the boggy hollow.

*Mayer Lake, Graham Island:*
Away from the crashing surf, there are quiet
waters, that reflect only the Loon's plaintive call.

*Grey Point, Moresby Island:*
The end of the road. Only a gaunt lightning
blasted stump and the wind.

*Tow Hill, Graham Island:*
A blow-hole roars and grunts in unison with the seas that mold and form the very rock.

*Gray Bay, Moresby Island:*
The storm washed in prodigious amounts of kelp,
some with floats like giant buoys and some like
ropes of pearls.

*Yan Village:*
A jade all-enveloping cloak of mosses illuminate the forest floor where once the *village of the proud eagle* stood.

*Skedans Village:*
Looking out through the encroaching forest, onto
deserted beaches that once echoed with a
thousand voices, the last standing poles keep a
lonely vigil.

*Skedans Village:*
The deep carvings made by the tools of man are
now overrun by natures rich colours.

*Skedans Village:*
The once proud giant red cedar house poles now
lie jumbled and rotting under a blanket of
luxurious mosses.

*Alliford Bay: mossy stump*
A simple stump, refuse from a careless industry, carried high on the beach by prodigious tides and seas, becomes itself a whole world of nature, in miniature.

*Tlell River:*
In the broad sweep of the stormy estuary, men
patiently stand like tiny birds at the waters edge.

*Queen Charlotte Seiner:*
Last light on a calm summer evening. Even the throb of the engine is muted.

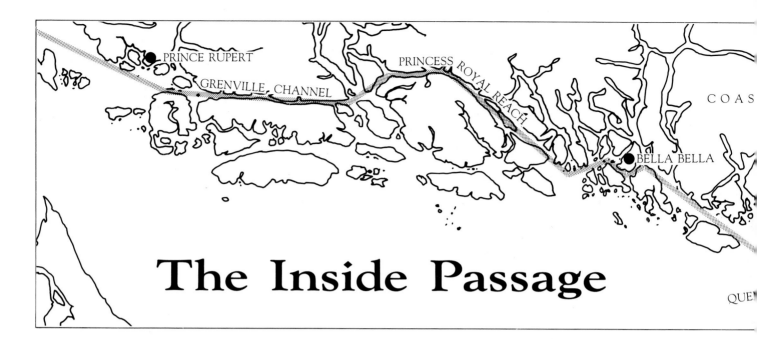

# The Inside Passage

1500 km northward from the Strait of Juan de Fuca to Skagway, Alaska, the Inside Passage threads through an incredible sequence of islands that shelter the mariner from the swells and uncertainties of the Pacific Ocean. These relatively quiet waters form a common chain, a bond, tying together a thousand communities with a water transportation system second in size to no other in the world.

Travelling north along the length of the Passage remarkable changes of scenery are easily observed as mild rain-shadow flora of the San Juan and Gulf Islands give way to the tall dark conifers and the gentle rolling land is replaced by ice-carved rocky peaks that crowd closer and closer to sea level until the glaciers themselves descend to the very water's edge. These, deep, swift and often tide-ripped waters, are the realm of leaping silver salmon and pods of orca, the killer whale, that draw excited shouts from their audiences at every lusty performance, while the sky above is dominated by slow circling bald eagles and the cry of the bold black raven.

Travelling the coast, whether on a short hop between islands, or wending one's way up the entire coast, is a wonderful experience. It's a chance to enjoy the freshness of the land around, discovering small communities and peoples with whom time passes gently. It is an opportunity to let go of the steering wheel, drink in the small details and observe a way of life measured with another scale as the ferries gently slip through narrow passes and channels and passengers feel so close to the land as they pass that they can almost reach out and touch the coves and cottages along the way. For those on longer journeys, well cared for staterooms can provide a private mural of delight and a shipboard atmosphere that stirs memories of long-forgotten or long-imagined ocean voyages.

But the enjoyment of water travel along the coast is not confined to the big vessels. Try the excitement of the local water-taxis, leaving from small bobbing village docks, loaded down with a fantastic jumble of bicycles, kids, coolers and the daily necessities of life for the local residents. They open up a whole new world of secluded beaches and scenic opportunity. And the Captains, no gold braid on these arms, a wonderful source of local lore and information, with tales to tell and often with schedules and routes of considerable flexibility.

Board one of the B.C. Ferries' ships at Port Hardy (Vancouver Island) and sail north across Queen Charlotte Strait, through Fitz Hugh Sound and Grenville Channel — an overnight trip of twenty hours to Prince Rupert on the mainland (Summer schedule). Or embark in Prince Rupert and make the trip in reverse. In winter the cruise departs Tsawwassen (35km

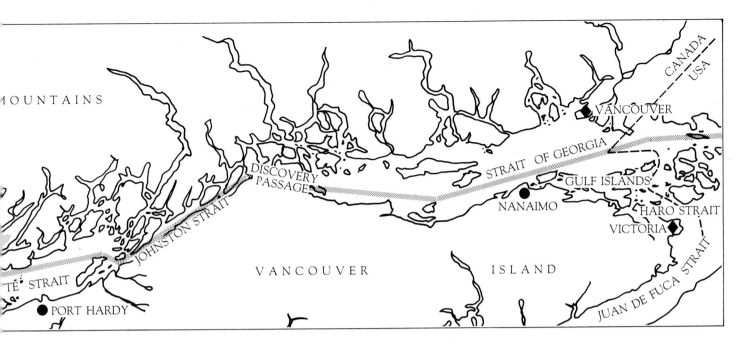

S. of Vancouver), stopping briefly in Port Hardy before continuing to Prince Rupert (34 hrs). Once a week the ship makes a 30-minute stop at the tiny coastal community of Bella Bella.

Reservations for vehicles and staterooms (if desired) should be made well in advance by phoning Vancouver ☎ (604)669-1211, or Victoria ☎ (604)386-3431; or by writing the B.C. Ferry Corporation, 1045 Howe Street, Vancouver, B.C. V6Z 2A9. The ferry systems are an extension of the highway network, and so your vehicle can travel along with you. Foot passengers may sleep on recliner chairs or on the covered deck if they do not wish staterooms. Public showers are available as well.

To travel to Port Hardy take one of the frequent Vancouver Island sailings to either Victoria or Nanaimo, and drive north along the scenic Island Highway (501km. from Victoria to Port Hardy, a drive of about 8 hrs). Or take the bus. There are a number of route variations. One could take the ferry from Vancouver (Horseshoe Bay) to Langdale, drive the Sunshine Coast to Powell River, board the ferry again to Comox on Vancouver Island, and drive north 294km. to Port Hardy.

With several days at your disposal consider returning from your cruise to Prince Rupert via the B.C. Interior. This route follows the Skeena River through the Bulkley Valley east for 721km. to Prince George. From here travel south along the historic Cariboo Highway, through the drier range country to Cache creek. Swing west on Highway 1 following the Thompson and then the Fraser rivers, through the spectacular Fraser Canyon, and finally through the Fraser Valley to Vancouver. Or from Prince Rupert take an Alaska State Ferry four day cruise even further north along protected waterways to Ketchikan, Wrangell, Petersburg, Juneau, and Skagway returning to either Prince Rupert or Seattle.

Passenger and vehicle reservations are a must. Stopovers may be made at no additional charge, but reservations should be made for departure from each stopover port. Write to Alaska Marine Highway, Pouch R, Juneau, Alaska 99811 or telephone Juneau ☎ (907) 465-3941 or Seattle ☎ (206)623-1970.

For alternate means of transportation to Prince Rupert and Port Hardy see the *How To Get There* section under those cities. Bus connections to Interior Alaska are provided by Alaska Yukon Motorcoaches ☎ Seattle (206)682-4101 or Anchorage (907) 276-1305. Connections to Interior Alaska and the Yukon are provided by White Pass and Yukon Motorcoaches ☎ Alaska (907) 277-5581, or toll free from outside ☎ (800) 544-2206.

# Queen Charlotte Islands

The *Misty Isles*, as this island chain is known, have about them a special aura and visitors might feel that these islands are themselves afloat, surrounded by their veils of legend and mystique. Visitors to these islands sense discovery, not only from a unique natural environment but also from the awsome cultural heritage of the native people and many bring back from their stay in the Queen Charlottes, elusive, enchanting experiences, that well may be addictive.

More than 100 kilometers offshore from the mainland of British Columbia, on the very edge of the continental shelf, the Queen Charlotte Islands were first sighted by the Spanish explorer Juan Perez in 1774. The archipelago consist of two major islands, Moresby and Graham, separated only by the slimmest slit of water and shaped together like a Stone Age arrowhead bulging to the North end where most of the population live. The abrupt San Cristoval mountain chain within the lower island, soaring from deep fjords on a wild and sea battered western shore, contains sawtooth peaks of 1000 metres and more, that cause dramatic and unpredictable fluctuations in the local weather and contribute to the rich and varied nature of the land.

Plants and animals of the Charlottes reflect the isolation of their habitat. In this unique environment, often called the *Canadian Galapogos*, natural growth has specialized in many different ways, to seemingly intrigue and confound the curiosity of biologists. For any observer, or naturalist, this richness is fully and immediatly felt and eight ecological reserves have been established to protect the delicate balances of things such as sea bird nesting grounds, sand dunes and the changing systems of bogs and forests.

These islands are the native home of the proud Haida native people, known for the aesthetics of their art and culture, their heroic prowess in intertidal warfare and their seafaring expertise in cedar dug-out canoes. The Haida's presence and history should be a major focus for visitors to these islands where traditions are being preserved in many ways. In the towns and villages a pride in the younger generation has been rekindled and older traditions, skill and the arts of their peoples are being taught with enthusiasm and vigour. The older and usually more remote villages, already plundered by museums and governments, succumb gradually to the vitality of the lush vegetation and are now carefully protected including a strict protocol that all visits to reserves and village sites be approved in advance by the Masset or Skidegate Band Council offices.

The journey by B.C. Ferries from Prince Rupert to Skidegate is somehow more of an adventure than most other coastal ferry rides. Leaving the calm of the Inside Passage's channel and waterways, the vessel heads out into the open Hecate Strait, with no sign of the destination ahead. The ocean swells off the Pacific make the boat feel small during the six hour sailing and first-timers peer anxiously forward for their first glimpse of landfall, a hazy blue mountainous outline.

Landing on Graham Island, the ferry docks in a small notch at the mouth of the island dotted Skidegate Inlet, this is the water that just a few miles away necks down to become a narrow roaring channel and swooshes westward out to the open ocean between Graham and Moresby Islands. A small B.C. Highways car ferry, the M.V. Kwuna links the two islands from the same terminal and provides convenient transportation south to Sandspit where it edges its way between low wooded islands and rocks into the tiny slip at its southern terminal.

Graham is a relatively flat island, with the fist of Masset Inlet thrust deep into its centre and Naikoon Provincial Park occupying the entire north-east quadrant. Miles of beaches and dunes border the wind-whipped forest and culminate at the far corner in the long sandy finger of Rose Spit. Many rivers, root-beer-coloured from the abundance of mosses that exhilarate in the mild, wet maritime climate, are magnet-like destinations for spawning salmon and fishermen rarely leave these parts without having caught their limit.

Moresby Island is becoming legendary for its remarkable unspoiled beauty and outstanding natural history. It is a mountainous island, sheltered on the eastern side with a wealth of islands and slashed by sounds and inlets in every direction. With only 15 km of paved roads, travellers must cautiously take to the logging roads to explore much of its natural beauty, where deer, full of curiosity, stand quietly along the roadside to watch you pass. The more extensive exploration of Moresby and surrounding islands, particularly the South Moresby Wilderness area, takes considerable and careful preparation calling for the use of boats and airplanes.

The island's main road connects the town of Queen Charlotte and the community at Skidegate Inlet in the south, with the major island commercial and population centre of Masset on the northern coast. The road provides breathtaking views of the driftwood-choked stormy beaches and passes tranquil, lily patterned, mirror-surfaced lakes, for those who delight in quieter waters. From Masset the deteriorating road enters the protection of a dappled primeval forest of moss-choked trees just a few meters away from the savage coastal surf and finally reaches its end on wide white beaches at Tow Hill, just beyond the location of the only organized campsite in the Charlottes.

*The Balancing Rock. As the tide rose, the rock seemed to move on the water's surface.*

Ninstints, on a small island close to the southern tip of the islands is the most extensive and certainly the most isolated Haida village site that has been preserved to date and now has been declared a World Heritage Site by UNESCO. Due to the remote location access is possible to this site only through a well organized group expedition. A dozen or more village sites are scattered around the islands, and an effort should be made by visitors to see at least one. Their remoteness enhances the step back in time that they induce on all who see them.

Logging and fishing are the Island's two major industries, both drawing upon the natural resources of the Charlottes. Tourism is still in the fledgeling or primitive stages of tapping a reclusive but world-class potential and tourists should not look for many of the normally expected amenities. A good rule for travellers would be to come to the islands prepared to be *self contained* as much as is practical during their stay. Some motel accommodation is available at several centres but many visitors come equipped to camp and take advantage of the solitude on empty and beautiful beaches.

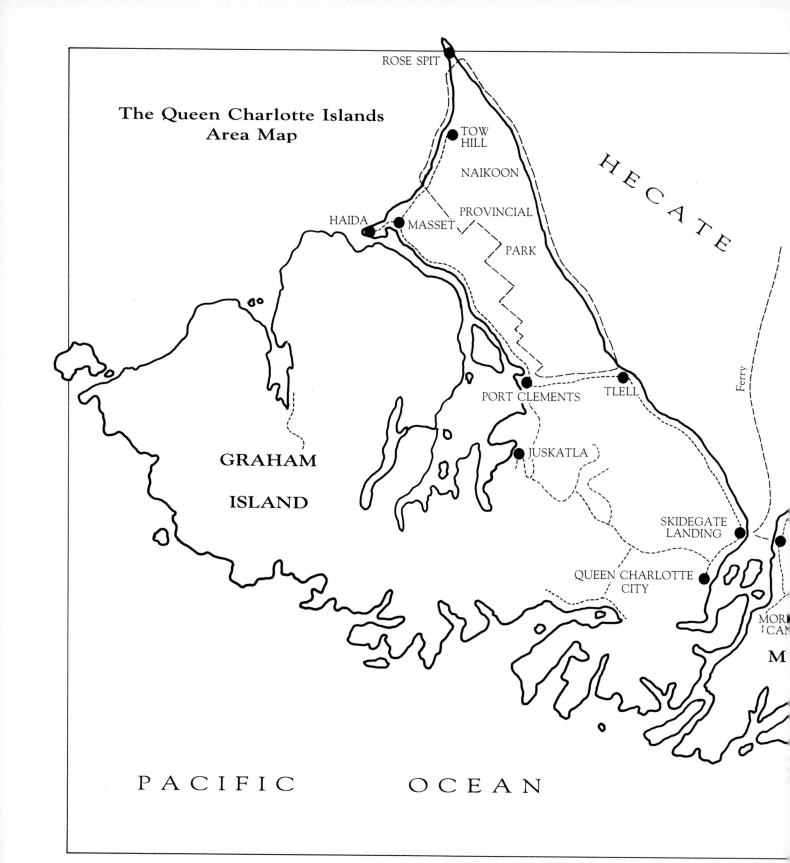

The Queen Charlotte Islands
Area Map

ROSE SPIT

TOW
HILL

NAIKOON

HAIDA

PROVINCIAL

MASSET

PARK

HECATE

GRAHAM

ISLAND

PORT CLEMENTS

TLELL

Ferry

JUSKATLA

SKIDEGATE
LANDING

QUEEN CHARLOTTE
CITY

MOR
CAN

M

PACIFIC          OCEAN

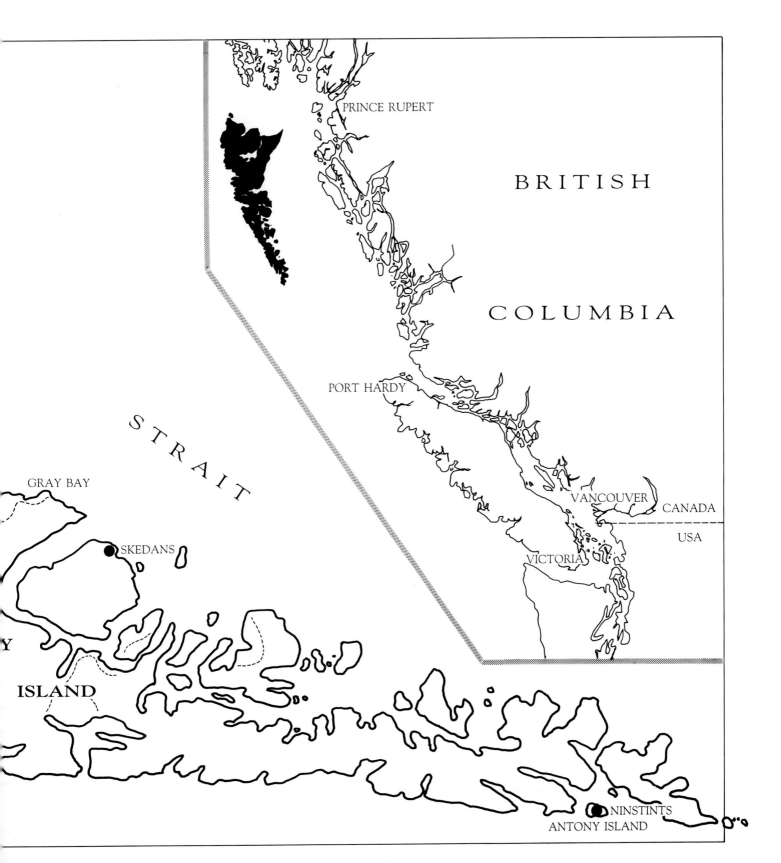

PRINCE RUPERT

BRITISH

COLUMBIA

STRAIT

PORT HARDY

GRAY BAY

SKEDANS

Y

ISLAND

VANCOUVER

CANADA

USA

VICTORIA

NINSTINTS
ANTONY ISLAND

## How to Get There.

**By Car:** From Prince Rupert via B.C. Ferries to Skidegate. Three times a week June through September; otherwise twice weekly. Reservations strongly recommended. Rivtow Straits Ltd. covered barge service Prince Rupert to Masset for vehicles and freight only (No passengers.) Twice weekly with connecting service to Vancouver. Reservations through B.C. Ferry Corp. Ministry of Highways ferry, M.V. Kwuna operates between Alliford Bay on Moresby Island and Skidegate on Graham Island, linking Sandspit Airport to the main roads on Graham. Hourly daytime sailings. **By Air:** Air B.C., Prince Rupert to all Queen Charlotte Is. points ☎ 627-1341 (Prince Rupert) North Coast Air Services, Prince Rupert to Masset ☎ 627-1351 (Prince Rupert) Pacific Western Airlines, Vancouver & Victoria to Sandspit- ☎ 684-6161 (Vanc.) or 388-5191 (Vict.) Trans Provincial Airlines, Prince Rupert to Sandspit, Masset, & Queen Charlotte City ☎ 627-1341 (Prince Rupert)

*Skidegate Inlet, filled with islands and dominated by misty mountains.*

## How To Get Around.

**Taxis:** in Sandspit, Skidegate, Queen Charlotte City, Port Clements, Masset & Haida. **Buses:** Claroth Enterprises operates between Sandspit Airport and Masset ☎ 626-5076 (Masset.) Mitco Marine operates between Sandspit Airport and Queen Charlotte City ☎ 559-8461 (Q.C.C.) **Bus Charter:** GRM Bus Services Ltd ☎ 559-4713 (Q.C.C.) **Car Rental:** Sandspit Airport – Budget, and Tilden Rent-a-Car. Queen Charlotte City Thrifty Rent-a-Car ☎ 559-8224; Tilden ☎ 559-8411. Masset – Budget ☎ 626-5571; Sears Rent-a-Car ☎ 626-3285. Cars, vans, pickups, & campers available. Reservations for summer and fall rentals are recommended. For those exploring by car, note there are about 160 kilometers (96 miles) of paved roads. Thousands of kilometers of secondary roads are privately owned by logging companies, and are accessible to the public on weekends and after working hours during the week. These roads must be used with caution. Information and maps can be obtained by contacting either MacMillan Bloedel Industries Limited at Juskatla, or Crown Zellerbach Canada limited at Sandspit.

## Where To Stay And Eat.

Hotel and motel accommodation in the various communities can be quite limited, so reservations are a must. In Sandspit, The Sandspit Inn ☎ 637-5334 is right at the airport, well maintained and a good location for travels on Moresby and southern Graham Island. On Graham Island itself, try the Singing Surf Inn ☎ 626-3318 at Masset and The Sea Raven Motel ☎ 559-4423 in Queen Charlotte City. There are several small lodges and houses for B. and B., but it is best to make local inquiries.

Camping is highly recommended to really get the feel of the islands. There are campsites at Mosquito Lake, Gray Bay and Copper Bay on Moresby Island, and at Pure Lake Park and Tow Hill on Graham Is. For the most part it is wilderness camping with many beautiful areas to choose from. Visitors are asked to respect private property, and to keep wilderness areas unspoiled. Carry proper clothing, provisions and equipment for complete outdoor living, including suitable maps. Bring large fresh water containers since many of the best campsites are without good drinking water.

## What To Do And See.

Fishing — salt and fresh water, angling, trolling, jigging, salmon, trout, steelhead, halibut, cod, crabbing and shellfish gathering. Hunting for deer, elk or black bear, grouse, and water fowl. Miles of sandy beaches provide a bonanza for rock hounds, beachcombers, photographers and those just interested in *getting away from it all.* Scuba diving and snorkeling are excellent in the clear waters. Visit Haida and Skidegate Mission, both reservation villages where native artists and artisans fashion exquisite gold and silver jewelry, argillite carvings, woven baskets, and silkscreened cloth. Or visit more remote abandoned village sites each with its remains of totems and longhouses. Note that permission to visit any of these remote sites must be obtained from the Haida Band Councils. Southern sites are under the jurisdiction of the Skidegate Band Council at Skidegate Mission ☎ 559-8306. For northern sites apply to Masset Band Council in Haida ☎ 626-3925. Access to these abandoned villages is by boat, charter boat or aircraft, or by educational tour. Wilderness expeditions from 2 to 10 days are available which include visits to ancient village sites, as well as other points of interest to the naturalist, photographer, or beachcomber. Contact Gwaii Watchmen, P.O. Box 1, RR 1, Skidegate, V0T 1S0; or Ecosummer Canada Expeditions, 1516 Duranleau St, Vancouver, V6H 3S4 to name just two. Moresby Is. is best explored by boat, while Graham Is. lends itself well to exploration by car or on foot. Points of interest are Tow Hill lookout, Delkatla Wildlife Sanctuary, Naikoon and Pure Lake Provincial Parks, the unique golden spruce tree and abandoned Haida dugout canoe south of Port Clements, the wreck of the Pesuta north of Tlell, and the Balancing Rock north of Skidegate. Be sure to visit the Queen Charlotte Islands Museum for displays of Haida art, pioneer and natural history. The Pallant Creek Salmon Hatchery welcomes visitors. Try Willows Golf Course, Skidegate ☎ 637-5472.

### Newspaper:

Queen Charlotte Islands Observer, Tlell. A useful publication for potential visitors is A Guide To The Queen Charlotte Islands, by Neil G. Carey, Alaska Northwest Publishing Company, Anchorage, Alaska 99509.

**Water Taxi:** Mitco Marine operates between Alliford Bay and Skidegate, and also charters to other points. **Boat Charters:** Mijo Service, Queen Charlotte City ☎ 559-4626; B. & K. Charters, Sandspit, spec. in fishing. ☎ 637-5395; Kallahin Expeditions Ltd, Queen Charlotte City, sightseeing, fishing. Also Island Bus Tours ☎ 559-4746; Misty Isles Expeditions, Sandspit, sightseeing, fishing. ☎ 637-5782; and others. **Boat Rental:** L & H Motors, Masset, small outboards. ☎ 626-3776. Boaters exploring on their own are advised a set of marine charts and tide tables are a necessity. Canadian Hydrographic Services provides a free catalogue of marine charts ("Information Bulletin #2".) The appropriate charts may then be purchased from them through the Institute of Ocean Sciences, P.O. Box 6000, Sidney B.C., V8L 4B2. **Diving Charter:** Q.C. Diving Enterprises Ltd, Queen Charlotte City, ☎ 559-4588. ☎ 626-3225; **Air Charter:** North Coast Air Service, Masset, Queen Charlotte Helicopters, Sandspit ☎ 637-5344; Trans Provincial Airlines, Sandspit ☎ 637-5355; Vancouver Island Helicopters, Sandspit ☎ 637-5665.

**For more information:** Queen Charlotte Islands Chamber Of Commerce, Box 357, Queen Charlotte, B.C., V0T 1S0, or Tourism British Columbia, 1117 Wharf Street, Victoria, B.C., V8W 2Z2.

# Prince Rupert

The silver ribbon of the Skeena river rushes headlong between a wild array of snowy summits, past thickly wooded islets and through land almost devoid of the heavy hand of civilization, to suddenly burst into the deep glacial coastal reaches at Prince Rupert.

This progressive city, a *City of Rainbows*, at the northern extreme of the British Columbia coast line, is the third largest ice-free harbour in Canada with its beginning dating back to the days of Charles M. Hays, Manager for the Grand Trunk Pacific railway, who strove to build a port to rival Vancouver. Today, Charles M. Hays' dream has been conceived, for the still-growing port of Prince Rupert serves as the most rapidly expanding port on the Pacific Coast of Canada. The city, which was named after the first governor of the first Hudson's Bay Company, is known as *The Gateway to the North*.

On a crisp day, beyond the local Mt. Hays (555 meters) can be seen, to the west, the Queen Charlottes Island's shimmer and to the north, the mountains of the Alaskan Panhandle. In this land of mountains and whimsicle shifting clouds the frequent rainbows bring character to this place. But, other than rainbows and freighters in the harbour Prince Rupert is reknowned as a hub of ferry and cruise ships plying the northern waters. The B.C. Ferries fleet here meets with the The Alaska State Ferries and dozens of Alaska cruise lines.

Visitors to the city should drop-in at the Visitor's Bureau/Museum to see, among many other things, an ancient rock petroglyph, a totem pole carved by legendary Chief Dudoward, and a carving shed where local artists labour as part of their cultural tradition.

Don't miss the flowers behind the courthouse at Service Park; one can appreciate that the sunken gardens that were originally intended to serve as the foundation for the Courthouse Building itself. Spectacular also are the foaming Butz Rapids formed by the fast waters coursing over the lip of Morse Basin; see them particularly on a falling tide. By visiting Oliver Lake one can witness how in a place like this it is not only man who sculpts the landscape; east of the lake flamboyant natural *bonsai* trees grow in gnarled shapes that have been determined by the soil and climate alone.

Not to be missed during a visit in the area are the incredible native villages and sites, mostly in the Hazelton area along the Skeena River. At Kispiox, a huge stand of totems are on display; at Ksan, a traditional native Indian village has been totally reconstructed. Throughout the surrounding area there are more than a dozen other very interesting preserved villages and historical sites.

## How To Get There

**B.C. Ferries** Port Hardy (Vancouver Island) to Prince Rupert, over night (15hrs, summer schedule); or Tsawwassen (Vancouver) via Port Hardy to Pr. Rupert (34hrs, Oct to May). See *Inside Passage*. Make car and stateroom reservations well in advance. B.C. Ferries Skidegate (Queen Charlotte Islands) to Pr. Rupert (8hrs). Car reservations. **Alaska Marine Highway** (Ferries) Seattle to Pr. Rupert; and South Eastern Alaska (Ketchikan, Juneau, Skagway and way points) to Pr. Rupert. See *Inside Passage*. Make reservations well in advance. **By Car:** Yellowhead Highway (No. 16) west from Edmonton and Prince George (721km from Prince George to Prince Rupert). **By Bus:** Greyhound Lines Vancouver or Edmonton via Pr. George to Pr. Rupert ☎ 683-9277 Vancouver. **By Train:** VIA Rail from Edmonton via Pr. George. ☎ (toll free) 112-800-665-8630. B.C. Rail Vancouver to Pr. George connecting with VIA Rail to Pr. Rupert. ☎ 987-6216 Vancouver. **By Air:** C.P. Air. ☎ 682-1411 Vancouver.

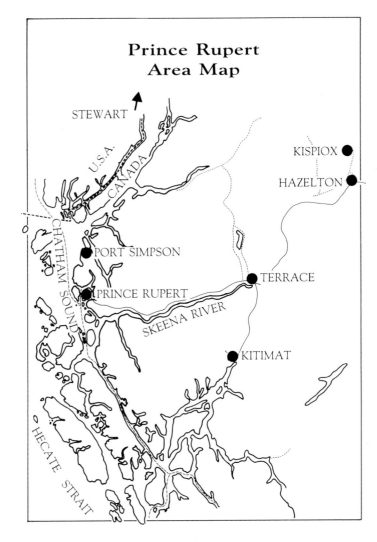

**Prince Rupert Area Map**

STEWART

KISPIOX

HAZELTON

PORT SIMPSON

TERRACE

PRINCE RUPERT

SKEENA RIVER

KITIMAT

U.S.A.

CANADA

CHATHAM SOUND

HECATE STRAIT

## How To Get Around

**Bus:** Prince Rupert City Transit. ☎ 624-3343. Farwest Bus Lines to Kitimat, Terrace, Airport limousine. ☎ 624-6400. **Taxi:** Skeena Taxi ☎ 624-2185; Reliable Cabs ☎ 624-9666. Prince Rupert Water Taxi ☎ 624-3337. **Car Rental:** Tilden ☎ 624-5318; Budget ☎ 627-7400; Sears ☎ 627-1701; and others. **Ferry:** Canadian III to Port Simson and Kincolith. B.C. Ferries, ☎ 624-9627 Pr. Rupert. **Boat charter/Rental:** Numerous, for fishing, diving, touring. Pick up a Charter Operator's Brochure or write to Prince Rupert Charter Operations, P.O. Box 1052, Prince Rupert, B.C., V8J 4H5. Also Dockside Boat Rentals ☎ 627-7786. **Air Charter:** Trans-Provincial Air ☎ 627-1341; Northcoast Air ☎ 627-1351. Check these airlines for scheduled local flights.

## Where To Stay And Eat

Numerous hotels and motels. Highliner Inn ☎ 624-9060, and Crest Motor Hotel ☎ 624-6771 both have a view of the harbour. Private campgrounds, as well as Prudhomme Lake Provincial campground. Approximately 40 restaurants to choose from with a wide selection of specialty foods served. Don't forget to sample the local fresh fish, it's available at many restaurant and worth seeking out.

## What To Do And See

Shop for local Indian crafts and art-masks, argillite carving, jewelry, and hand knits at Harbour Crafts or Museum of Northern B.C. Take a walking tour of the city, tour the city's modern and prestigious harbour, or ride on the Mount Hays Sky Ride. See Butze Reversing Rapids, Diana Lake (good for a cool dip on a Summer's day) and Oliver Lake Provincial Parks. Take a tour of a fish cannery, grain terminal or pulp mill. Canoe the local rivers. If you have a little more time travel the wild and scenic Skeena River Valley, or take the worth while trip to the reconstructed K'san Indian village at the junction of the Bulkley and Skeena Rivers through Allwest Tours ☎ 624-2778. They also offer air tours of the Cambria Icefields or the Queen Charlotte Islands.

The waters around Prince Rupert are reknowned for their fishing excellence. Ardent fishermen should take the time to charter a boat and get out to where the big ones are waiting.

Check out the art gallery, the Indian and local historic displays at the Museum of Northern B.C., Indian carving at the Carving Shed, on your city walking tour, where native carvers create their traditional crafts, and fishing exhibits at the Northcoast Marine Museum. There are a variety of recreational and sports facilities including The Centennial Golf Course. Local Celebrations include Charlie Hays Days March; Sea Fest June; Folk Festival July 1st. weekend. *The Prince Rupert Daily News* is published 5 times per week and is a great source of information on local happenings.

**Visitors Information** Box 660, Prince Rupert, B.C. ☎ 624-5637.

# A Cruise to Alaska

*Fishing Lures:*
The fish boats are decked out with their finest
jewels flashing in the sun.

*Fishing Floats:*
Colourful floats shout their numbers from boat to boat over the tangle of netting and lines.

*Fallen Leaf:*
Nature mimics our careful art, so simply.

*Ketchikan, Saxman Totem Park:*
In a wood banked boundary a saucy frog's face,
freshly made up, invites us inside.

*Wrangell:*
With distances so large between communities,
many local inhabitants rely on the float plane for
their daily needs.

*Ketchikan:*
Beneath the austere mist enveloped mountains,
alpine meadows lead close to the shore where
floating houses gently move.

*Alaska, Inside Passage:*
The flickering light through the short summer
night.

*Alaska, Inside Passage:*
The sun seemed to hesitate, reluctant to leave the sky, and a late fisherman hurried home.

*Artist, Ketchikan:*
Restoration of native art is an important step in
keeping the culture alive and growing.

*Shakes Island, Wrangell:*
Over a piled causeway, surrounded by bobbing boats, Chief Shakes Island is studded with totem poles.

*The Inside Passage:*
A first ferry ride, like a first party, is a memory
never to be forgotten. How big the ship seemed
and how quickly time passed by.

*The Road to Alaska:*
A ferry's wash leaves implanted on the surface of the sea a trail of textured foam swelling like our journeys memories.

# A Cruise To Alaska

## The Alaska Marine Highway

Just a few steps at Prince Rupert connect passengers on the British Columbia Ferries network with the Southeast portion of the Alaska Marine Highway system, a true extension of the road network, linking many of the coastal cities and towns through a fleet of ferries designed for both passengers and vehicles. Ports of call include Ketchikan, Hollis, Wrangell, Petersburg, Kake, Sitka, Angoon, Tenakee, Hoonah, Juneau, Haines and Skagway in Alaska, as well as Prince Rupert, B.C. and Seattle in Washington.

The schedule operates from the beginning of May to the end of September with reservations a must and preferably made well in advance. Standby space is available on a first come basis, but travellers on standby status risk being off-loaded at each port of call.

Reservations may be made for two, three, or four-berth cabins with complete facilities or, for those willing to share a cabin, berths are available for dormitory-style accommodation. Stopovers may be made at no additional charge, but reservations should be made for departure from each stopover port.

Forest Service naturalist-interpreters aboard ship present comprehensive programs and information concerning the forested waterways through the Chugach and Tongass National Forests describing the surroundings and wildlife.

For complete information, schedules, and reservations write Alaska Marine Highway, Pouch R, Juneau, Alaska 99811; or telephone Juneau ☎ (907)465-3941 or Seattle ☎ (205)623-1970.

## Alaska Jetfoil Service.

For those wishing to travel at greater speeds this jetfoil service operates between Skagway, Haines, Juneau, Hoonah, Tenakee, Angoon and Sitka from mid-June to the beginning of September. Call toll free from Alaska and Continental U.S. ☎ 800-621-5598, or from Washington State ☎ 800-421-1825.

## Cruises And Cruisetours.

A bewildering number of cruises, both luxury and otherwise, are available from May through September and more are being added all the time. A new class of vessels, mini-cruisers, are becoming popular, carrying only a hundred or so passengers and offering a much more intimate view of glacier strewn fjords; their unique bow ramps allow passengers to disembark for sightseeing and exploring in more remote areas: other larger vessels offer the opportunity for taking your vehicles along with you. A number of lines have cruisetour packages which include greater distances and more varied scenery by adding other modes of travel — air, motorcoach and, in some cases, rail — for some sections of the tour. Other options offered include air flights to points within the Artic Circle, or a day's travel by train through Denali National Park and several companies include Anchorage and Central Alaska plus Whitehorse, Yukon in their itinerary. Alternatively there are one-way trips either north or southbound and, of course, the length of the tour may vary from several days to several weeks. Cruises commence from such diverse ports as Los Angeles, San Francisco, Seattle, Vancouver, Prince Rupert, Ketchikan and Skagway. You will need a travel agent to get full details and listings.

## Ketchikan.

The first Alaska port for northbound vessels, Ketchikan, perched on the slopes of Deer Mountain, snakes along the shore of Revillagigedo Island sentried by the totem poles of Totem Bight State Park to the north and Saxman Totem Park to the south. Salmon struggle up the tumbling creek water alongside the boardwalk house right downtown. A tour of the city always includes picturesque and infamous Creek Street, built on "stilts" out over the bay and currently being restored. Visit too, the Frontier Saloon with its local stage production, the Tongass Historical Society Museum (pioneer and Alaskan Indian artifacts and art works), the Deer Mountain Fish Hatchery, Totem Heritage Centre and, of course, Totem Bight Historical Site for the wonderful display of totems complete with Indian Longhouse. Designs of the poles proclaim statements, or stories and a curious pole at Saxman is topped by a figure of President Lincoln.

Cruises to Misty Fjords National Monument are available from Ketchikan. The MV Chilkat serves the Indian town of Metlakatla on Annette Island. Unfortunaty however the dramatic scenery in the Misty Fjords National Monument can only be seen through plane or boat charters.

## Wrangell.

At the delta of the majestic Stikine River, Wrangell was once Fort Dionysius of imperial Russia and was also under the Union Jack for a while before flying the American Stars and Stripes. The wealth of seal and sea otter furs was the initial reason for settlement on Wrangell Island. Then, gold rushes in the late 1800's shaped Wrangell to be an important crossroad. The Tlingit native people tell that they arrived to this place in canoes by daring to go under the ice of a glacier on the river.

Wrangell is noted for its collection of totems and its Indian tribal house. The poles and Chief Shake's House on Chief Shake's Island can be visited by crossing a stilted walkway. The islet is circled by the activities of busy fish-boats. Petroglyphs on the beaches are estimated to be over 8000 years old but will probably keep their mystery. Wrangell Museum contains a good display of Tlingit artifacts, petroglyphs and local historical items.

A particular ledge where semi-precious garnets are embedded in the rock had been bequeathed to the children of Wrangell and young entrepreneurs make shipboard visits to entice passengers with their stones.

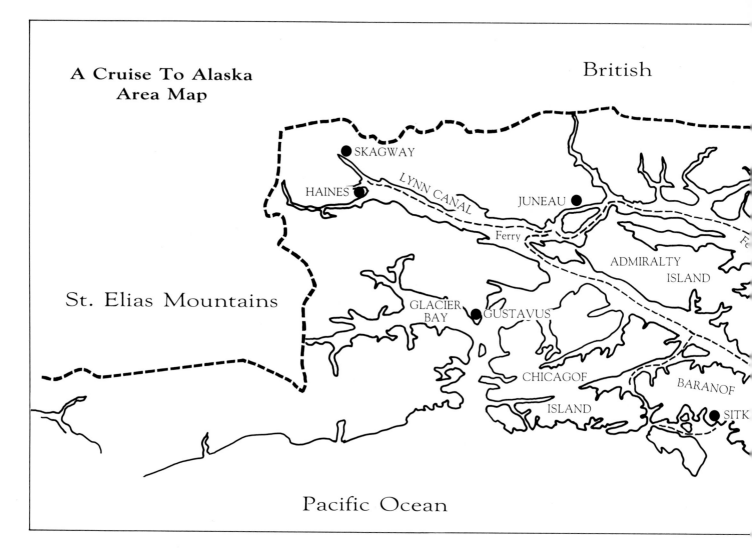

**A Cruise To Alaska Area Map**

British

SKAGWAY

HAINES

LYNN CANAL

JUNEAU

Ferry

ADMIRALTY ISLAND

St. Elias Mountains

GLACIER BAY

GUSTAVUS

CHICAGOF

ISLAND

BARANOF

SITK

Pacific Ocean

## Petersberg

Immediately south of Petersberg, ferries negotiate 22 miles of the Wrangell Narrows that is a mere 300 ft wide at the slimmest point where ferries needs a certain tide level in order to navigate through and are guided by a series of markers. Sometimes sailing schedules need to be adjusted according to the tides.

Petersberg is the *Little Norway* of Alaska and a hospitable community. The Norwegian Independence Festival in May is an exuberant Viking celebration. Processing of salmon, halibut, shrimp, crab and scallops can be viewed at the canneries, with the Petersberg shrimp considered the local specialty.

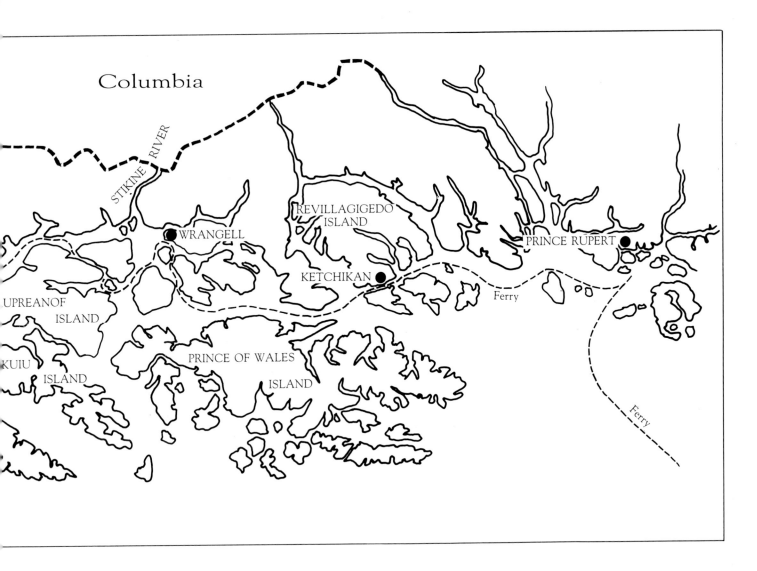

Columbia

STIKINE RIVER

WRANGELL

REVILLAGIGEDO ISLAND

KETCHIKAN

PRINCE RUPERT

Ferry

UPREANOF ISLAND

KUIU ISLAND

PRINCE OF WALES

ISLAND

Ferry

## Sitka

On the west coast of Baranof Island, Sitka's harbour is only shielded from the Pacific Ocean by small islands. Framed by the symmetrical volcanic cone of Mt. Edgecumbe, Sitka has had a significant role in the history of Alaska.

Sitka, for half a century the center of Russian fur trade on this continent, still retains some of its ethnic past and the Russian influences remain visible in some of the buildings. Tlingit Indians made adamant resistances to the first Russian fur trading settlements and it was in Sitka that the official transfer of Alaska from Russia to the United States took place; that event is re-enacted on Alaska Day in October. Visit the Rus-

sian Bishop's House, St. Michael's Cathedral (extensive collection of Russian Orthodox art and artifacts), the Isabelle Miller Museum, and the Sheldon Jackson College and Museum (Eskimo and Indian tools and relics plus Russian memorabilia). A must for all visitors is a performance by the colourful costumed New Archangel Russian Dancers.

Sitka Busline offers tours for cruise and ferry passengers. Nearby Sitka National Historical Park has an excellent collection of Tlingit and Haida totems, while native crafts are demonstrated in the Southeast Alaskan Indian Cultural Centre.

Beautiful, and lively in its preservation of a fascinating history, Sitka rests warmly in the memories of visitors. It is called the *Pearl of the Pacific*.

## Juneau

Alaska's capital city, manages to mix sophistication with the colour of the frontier town. Juneau sits nestled on a mountainside, the gold-town history still clings on with narrow streets and frontier-style saloons, while alpine peaks and meadows, waterfalls, wetlands and the Mendenhall Glacier are all within walking distances. During the summer, ferries dock at Auke Bay which curves below the blue-white river of ice.

A one hour self-guided walking tour of the city covers such diverse points of interest as the State Capital Building and its fine viewing terrace, the old St. Nicholas Russian Orthodox Church, the House of Wickersham with its original furnishings and pioneer artifacts, the Alaska State Museum of Eskimo and Indian relics with its natural history exhibits and the sawdust-strewn Red Dog Saloon! Boats for fishing or sightseeing may be chartered, or bus tours taken to the nearby ice fields. Hiking, gold panning or visiting old mine ruins, river float trips, and glacier walks are all available. Juneau icefields flights may be arranged locally through several charter companies and a tour to Mendenhall Glacier in the Tongass National Forest is a memorable one.

## Haines

Up the Lynn Canal, situated on the beautiful Chilkat Peninsula, Haines is the ancestral home of the Chilkat Tlingit Indians. Nearby, a rare sight, thousands of bald eagles converging to feed along a section of the Chilkat River that does not freeze over. Haines features the Sheldon Museum and Cultural Centre with its displays of Alaskan artifacts. Nearby, in the old port of Chilkoot, is Fort William H. Seward with its replica of an Indian village, and its centre for native carvers. Chilkat Indian dances are performed several times a week, as are stage performances of an historic comedy.

Haines is the junction of ferry traffic and the most direct highway to interior Alaska. The highway passes Canada's Kluane National Park which is a World Heritage Site.

*Ketchikan, the gateway to Alaska.*

## Glacier Bay

From Juneau, many excursions are made to Glacier Bay, where the glaciers rumble into the sea and humpback whales, killer whales and seals may be cavorting among the icebergs. Glacier Bay is probably Alaska's premiere attraction with its 16 active tidewater glaciers and many more hanging glaciers. Black bear, brown bear and mountain goat are among the prolific land-based wildlife.

## Skagway

Arriving at Skagway is like walking into gold rush history. For this was the jumping off point for the thousands of Klondike gold seekers; here miners and pioneers tackled the tortuous Chilkoot Trail to reach the riches of the Yukon. Part of town is now preserved as the Klondike Gold Rush National Historic Park. Take a walking tour through the cemetery where notorious Soapy Smith and his adversary Frank Reid were buried after a mutually disastrous gunfight, or walk the main street with its old false-fronted buildings and boardwalks. Take in the Klondike-style stage show at the Eagles Hall with singing, dancing and "gambling". Visit the Trail of '98 Museum for its display of native and gold rush artifacts.

Skagway, at the head of Taiya Inlet, is the northern terminus for the Alaska Marine Highway System and the final destination of the Inside Passage. The link to Whitehorse is now opened by the Klondike Highway.

## Prince of Wales Island

Alaska Ferries reach Prince of Wales Island at Hollis, and less frequently, the isolated villages of Kake, Angoon, Hoonah and Tenakee Springs. Periodically a ferry goes to the tiny place of Pelican.

*above:*

*At Prince Rupert, the B.C. Ferry meets the Alaska Marine Highway.*

*below:*

*Wrangell's old stilted houses along the waterfront.*

# Index Of Place Names

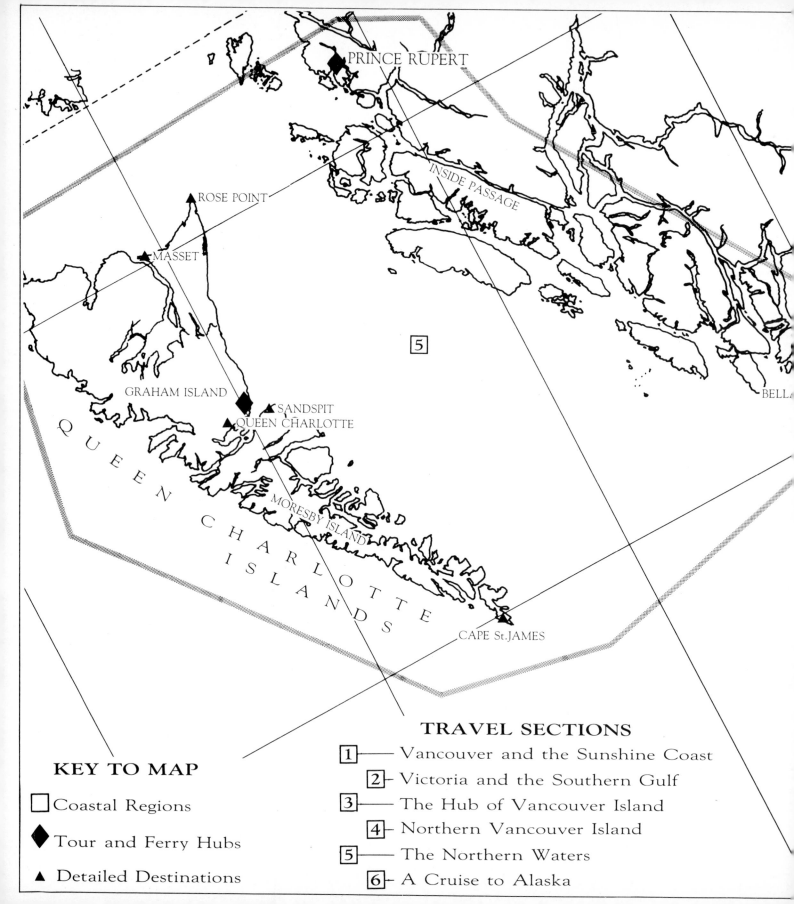

PRINCE RUPERT

INSIDE PASSAGE

ROSE POINT

MASSET

GRAHAM ISLAND

5

BELLA

SANDSPIT
QUEEN CHARLOTTE

Q U E E N   C H A R L O T T E   I S L A N D S

MORESBY ISLAND

CAPE St. JAMES

## TRAVEL SECTIONS

| 1 | — Vancouver and the Sunshine Coast |
| 2 | — Victoria and the Southern Gulf |
| 3 | — The Hub of Vancouver Island |
| 4 | — Northern Vancouver Island |
| 5 | — The Northern Waters |
| 6 | — A Cruise to Alaska |

## KEY TO MAP

☐ Coastal Regions

◆ Tour and Ferry Hubs

▲ Detailed Destinations